CFA Exam Audio Study Guide! Level 1 - Best Test Prep Book to Help You Pass the Test Complete Review & Practice Questions to Become a Chartered Financial Analyst!

content within this book, without the consent of the author or publisher.

Disclaimer Notice:
Please note the information contained within this document is for educational and entertainment purposes only. All effort has been executed to present accurate, up to date, and reliable, complete information. No warranties of any kind are declared or implied. Readers acknowledge that the author is not engaging in the rendering of legal, financial, medical or professional advice. The content within this book has been derived from various sources. Please consult a licensed professional before attempting any techniques outlined in this book.

By reading this document, the reader agrees that under no circumstances is the author responsible for any losses, direct or indirect, which are incurred as a result of the use of information contained within this document, including, but not limited to, — errors, omissions, or inaccuracies.

Table of Contents

Introduction

In your pursuit of excellence in financial investment, one of the top designations you should seek is the Chartered Financial Analyst (CFA). This charter is not just an accomplishment, it is a prestigious award. It is not one of the easiest designations to earn. It takes sheer dedication and determination to go through all the levels and eventually become a CFA charter holder. The charter demands endurance and in-depth knowledge of investment and financial markets. Other than your knowledge, this process tests your will, wit, diligence and endurance.

One of the best things about the CFA is that it is a program you can study while self-teaching as you prepare for the exam. The CFA Institute has structured the program in such a way that students from all walks of life can benefit through distance learning. While there are three levels, Level I, Level II and Level III, our emphasis in this book will be Level I. Before you are awarded the CFA charter, you have to pass all levels and meet some professional criteria.

Each year there are hundreds of thousands of students who enroll into the CFA program. Everyone has their reasons for enrolling. The CFA charter prepares you for some wholesome changes in your life and career. The decision to pursue this charter should primarily be influenced by your chosen career path. Professionals in the financial industry hold the CFA charter in high regard. Some of the individuals who will find this useful include relationship managers, research analysts, portfolio managers, fund managers, financial managers, and strategists.

The CFA charter is not just for financial professionals. Beyond the financial industry, attorneys and accountants can also enroll for the CFA in a bid to widen their knowledge on financial matters and precedence.

Level I is generally your foray into the financial markets. This study guide will help you prepare for your exam by covering the key study areas. We have included a study notes summary in each chapter, which you can brush through to get a grip of the content before you jump into the questions and answers. The question style is typical of what you will find on the exam. Therefore, going through these questions will give you that examination feeling.

The answers are adequately explained, helping you understand the reasoning behind them. From the question and answer structure, you will learn how to choose the right answer from a selection of multiple-choice answers.

You have to approach the exam with a sharp mind. Some of the questions contain answers that are all correct. However, only one of the answers precisely answers the question. Try to read and understand each question carefully so that you comprehend what it demands, and respond accordingly.

This study guide covers all the sections you will encounter in the exam, according to their examination weight. Your six-hour exam includes 240 multiple questions, split equally between the early morning session and the afternoon session. As you go through the questions in this book, remember to train yourself on time management. Ideally, you should not spend more than 90 seconds on a question.

This study guide will cover the following areas:

Ethics and Professional Standards

The focus of this chapter is on ethics, professional standards and the Global Investment Performance Standards (GIPS). This is one of the sections that demands most of your attention given that the CFA Institute gives it utmost attention, too. Your understanding of this section is critical because it helps to prepare you for Level II and Level III.

Quantitative Methods

In this chapter, you will draw on your knowledge of statistics and statistical methods. This is the first point where you interact with some math, and it might be a daunting task for students who do not find math very enjoyable. The emphasis in this chapter is on your understanding of analytical tools necessary for managing equities, portfolios and fixed income.

Economics

Your understanding of microeconomic and macroeconomic concepts will be tested in this section. You should have an easier experience if you have a background in economics, especially when dealing with macroeconomic concepts. Learn about the important graphs, because if there is one thing you can always be sure about in economics, it's that no exam is complete without a few questions that demand your interpretation of graphs.

Financial Reporting and Analysis

More than 20% of your exam will come from this section, hence it is widely considered the largest and probably one of the most important sections of the paper. Everything you learn in this chapter will come in handy as you prepare for the advanced levels in your course. You must have working knowledge of the cash flow statement, income statement and the balance sheet. Beyond that, understand the financial ratios, and the different ways assets and liabilities are treated and accounted for under IFRS or GAAP.

Corporate Finance

This section is relatively short and will primarily cover topics around agency operations, like capital budgeting, managing working capital, the relationship between principal investors and agency investors, and cost of capital.

Portfolio Management

This section is self-explanatory, and is about managing portfolios. In-depth knowledge of the

Capital Asset Pricing Model (CAPM) and Modern Portfolio Theory should help you ease through it. The information in this section will also help you set the foundation for advanced CFA levels.

Equity Investments

This section is primarily about company and security valuation and analysis. Most of the questions are on equities and decisions investors and investment managers make regarding the securities held.

Fixed Income

In this section, your understanding of fixed income securities and their prices will be tested. Knowledge of structured products like mortgage obligations will also make your work easier as you wade through fixed income markets and the instruments used in investing in these markets.

Derivatives

This section introduces you to investment vehicles that derive their value from other items in the market, like options, swaps, futures and forwards. It will only take up 5% of the questions.

Alternative Investments

This section is more about your understanding of concepts above anything else. It deals with unique investment options like investing in distressed securities, hedge funds, real estate or the commodities market.

CFA questions are mostly logical. The choices are arrived at following some of the common mistakes that students make either in their calculations, or in their understanding of the logical construct behind the statements. As you read through this book, make sure you familiarize yourself with the main calculator functions. This knowledge will come in handy in some of the questions on your exam. There are many reasons why this charter is important to you, hence the need to get a quality study guide that can help you prepare adequately for the exam. Enrolling for the CFA charter is an affordable option compared to undertaking an MBA. There is more value in the CFA, and the fact that you can study part-time while keeping up with your daily schedule makes this one of the best options you can consider.

When you are awarded the CFA charter, you will be joining an elite team of more than a hundred thousand financial experts all over the world. The representation spans 135 countries, so you are in very good company. This charter is not just about passing an exam and getting an award, it is primarily about value addition in your company. By enhancing your knowledge of the financial and investment markets, you are in a good position to aim for promotions or better career offers in the industry.

On average, individuals who complete the CFA charter have a better shot at negotiating higher earnings in their companies. The wealth of knowledge in your possession makes you an industry expert, and you will be sought after by some of the top companies. There are more opportunities for you in finance and investment once you earn your CFA charter.

This book will help you build your comprehension and basic knowledge of important portfolio management and investment valuation topics. The CFA Level I exam is properly balanced to give you a good introduction into the world of financial and investment markets. Of course, some of the topics and questions will take significantly longer than others, but try to make sure you apportion your time accordingly. With a study guide, you can learn and prepare yourself adequately.

Chapter 1: Ethical and Professional Standards

One of the most important expectations of a financial analyst is to uphold the utmost ethical values as you go about your activities. Ethical and professional standards go over and above any regulations, laws and rules set in the market. They affect careers, and lives, especially in instances where the law is not clear on what to do. As a financial analyst, you must be a responsible individual, and carry out your mandate in a professional manner.

Ethics and Trust in Financial Investment

Every decision in your line of work will affect groups and individual stakeholders directly or indirectly. Ethical principles are also referred to as moral principles. They are a reflection of the acceptable behavior expected of an analyst. These are moral principles that guide the industry. A code of ethics is a written set of rules and principles that become the norm. They are the foundation of interaction in the organization.

As a CFA, you are a professional, which means the following:

You have unique skills and knowledge

You offer services to others

You abide by a code of ethics as you carry out your mandate

In light of the statements above, the CFA has guidelines on the standard of conduct, and more importantly, consequences for failing to adhere to the said standards. It is important to establish these standards and consequences, because any violation does not just affect the individual, but the entire community.

For example, as a CFA, you must hold the interests of clients and the investment profession above your personal interests. You are also expected to make full disclosure of any information that might affect the objectiveness of the financial statements you handle.

CFA is built around integrity, honesty, diligence, transparency, and putting the client's needs above yours. Each year, you might be expected to reaffirm your commitment and compliance to the Code and Standards to ensure that the CFA community is made up of responsible professionals.

While you might strive to conduct yourself in a professional way, you might encounter situations where the law or course of action is not clearly defined. This presents a challenge to your ethical being.

One of the biggest challenges people face is that they have a natural assumption that they hold the highest ethical standards. This fallacy creates an element of overconfidence, which impairs your judgement.

Situational influences are another challenge that impedes your ability to act within the right ethical confines. These are situations where external factors conspire to influence your decision making, such as the allure of prestige or money, bonuses, employer loyalty and promotions. These influences blind you to the important factors in your analysis. Serious firms should come up with astute compliance programs to ensure their teams follow strict policies, regulations, and rules as they go about their business.

The investment industry is a supply and demand industry, matching capital suppliers to demand for financing in different capacities. Investors hope that they spend their money on ventures that will yield returns, and be well-compensated for taking a risk on their investment. When ethical standards are upheld, the flow of information and capital is flawless. It breeds trust, which is important for confidence building in firms, society, individuals, and the financial markets.

It is commonplace for people to invest in a venture when they believe the venture is trustworthy. This way, money is kept in circulation, which is good for the economy in general. Without trust, people withdraw their money from investments, and would rather keep it in their accounts or spend it.

The investment market is full of intangible investments. As a result, they can only be seen in the manner that the analysts present them, as facts and figures. Investors, therefore, rely on such information to select their investment machinery. Without trust, these investments can never take place.

Financial markets, therefore, are built upon trust and ethical standards. They encourage participation in the markets, in the hope that more opportunities for investment arise for investors. While legal standards are often set in different jurisdictions, ethical codes of conduct go over and above the standards, especially where the law is not very clear.

Code of Ethics and Professional Conduct

The CFA Institute understands that the importance of understanding and enforcing the code of ethics and professional conduct in normal professional circumstances, hence the official handbook to guide analysts. Any candidate or member that enrolls to the CFA program must comply with the code and standards applicable.

Candidates and members are expected to report annually on any matter that brings their conduct into question, like any involvement in litigation or criminal investigations. They should also expect investigation into their professional conduct in the event of a formal written complaint against them. Members of CFA staff should also note that the CFA Institute is always on the lookout for unfavorable conduct by any members, reported through different outlets, including social media. All of this is to make sure that members undertake their duties with integrity. According to the CFA Institute, all members, including charter holders and candidates, are expected to:

Work towards maintaining and improving their professional competence.

Conduct themselves with diligence, competence, respect and integrity.

Promote the viability and integrity of the capital markets.

Place the interests and integrity of their profession and clients above their personal interests.

Encourage ethical and professional behavior in relation to the profession.

Exercise care in independent judgement when engaging in professional activities.

The Standards of Professional Conduct

Professionalism

You are expected to understand and uphold the law, rules, and regulations applicable to your jurisdiction at all times. This includes licensing and regulatory requirements.

Members must act in a logical manner, exercising reasonable judgement and care to ensure objectivity and independence as they undertake their professional roles.

You must not misrepresent yourself, actions, recommendations or analysis.

You must not engage in any unprofessional conduct such as deceit, fraud, dishonesty or any criminal act that might reflect adversely on your professional integrity, competence or reputation.

Capital market integrity

You must never act on material nonpublic information and use it to influence an investment. Members must never engage in any activity that could result in price manipulation or affect the trading volume of an investment instrument.

Duties to clients

You must be loyal to your clients. This includes conducting yourself in a careful and prudent manner, putting the needs of your clients above yours.

You should interact with all clients objectively and in fairness. You must not appear to favor some clients over others.

In an advisory capacity with your clients, you must advise the client accordingly, by first determining whether their intended investment is suitable to their current financial position. Second, you must ensure you are aware of the client's experience in investments, their risk exposure and objectives. Finally, make sure you advise them on suitable investments in light of their portfolio.

When handling a client's portfolio, you must act in a manner that is consistent with the client's objectives and honor the portfolio constraints.

All information about your clients, present, past or prospective, must be handled with confidentiality unless disclosure is legally warranted, or unless the client allows.

Always do your best to present quality, accurate, and actionable information to clients at all times.

Duties to employers

In your capacity as a supervisor, you must ensure all members of staff under you comply with the required laws, codes and standards as stipulated in their professional code of conduct.

You must not accept compensation, gifts, benefits or any other form of consideration that results in a conflict of interest, unless there is written proof of clear intention from everyone involved.

Your activities will solely be for the benefit of your current employer. In this case, you must never act in any manner that might interfere with your employer's practice.

Investment analysis

Exercise due diligence during investment analysis, especially when offering recommendations and conclusions.

When communicating with prospective and current clients, you must provide all the necessary information they need to help them make sound investment choices. You must also inform them of the challenges and risks involved in their investment.

You must use your capacity as a professional to show the client the difference between opinions and facts.

You must always keep and maintain all relevant records pertaining to transactions involving your clients' investments and communication.

Conflict of interest

Should you be in a position that induces conflict of interest, you must disclose this and all pertinent information that might affect your judgement.

Investment transactions concerning your employers or clients must always take precedence over transactions that benefit you personally.

You must disclose any form of compensation received or paid to third parties for referrals.

Personal responsibilities as a CFA

You must conduct yourself in such a manner that you do not compromise your professionalism, integrity or that of the CFA Institute as you go about your daily activities.

Global Investment Performance Standards (GIPS)

In order to get the best investment objectives, investors must look at present and past performance of investment managers to ensure they have the right person for the job. The GIPS standards are a set of ethical principles that create a standardized approach that can be used to deliver the best investment returns to clients.

The GIPS standards also promise full disclosure and fair representation to clients in the course of investment performance, thereby ensuring that management firms and individuals do not engage in misrepresentation or any other act that might prevent them from behaving in the best interest of their clients.

Compliance with the GIPS standards is voluntary, not a legal requirement from regulatory bodies. To claim compliance, the firm must be managing actual assets. This means consultants and plan sponsors are not eligible to claim compliance, unless they manage the assets over which they intend to claim compliance.

Compliance is applicable all across the management firm, and not to specific products or composite products. With this in mind, firms can either claim compliance, or choose not to.

GIPS standards are created to protect prospective clients and investment management firms. Compliant management firms assure clients that they have a good historical record, and fair representation.

Compliant firms can engage in and place bids against other firms all over the world. Through compliance, firms can also ensure they have astute policies and procedures, setting them a bar above the rest.

In the case of investors, compliance bestows confidence in the investment firms they engage. It allows them to compare performance between different compliant management firms.

Composites

Composites refer to a collection of portfolios being managed under a specific strategy, objective, or investment mandate. This could include discretionary, fee-paying, or actual portfolios, as long as they are held under the same investment strategy. Any management firm must determine the right criteria for determining the portfolios to hold in a composite beforehand.

Verification

Compliant firms must be held accountable for their claims, and maintaining compliance. Since firms self-regulate in terms of compliance claims, it is reasonably expected that they involve third parties to verify their compliance, and strengthen their claim.

Verification is important to the entire firm because it helps to determine whether the firm complies with the GIPS standards, and whether the necessary procedures and policies are adhered to. The following conditions must be met for verification to take place:

It can only be done by an independent and qualified third party.

Verification must determine whether the investment firm meets the minimum requirements for composites as per the GIPS standards.

A verification report must be issued for the entire firm, not just part or composite.

Firms can be verified if they have been around for no less than one year.

Importance of GIPS standards

Investment firms need GIPS standards for the following reasons:

Global outreach

With the GIPS standards applicable, the investment firm assures the clients that their portfolios are managed by an astute and credible investment firm. It is easier for investment firms, even small firms that have limited investment performance standards, to compete in the global markets with companies that are more established all over the world.

Measure of performance

GIPS also help investment firms to compete on a global scale, given that the industry is growing worldwide in terms of financial instruments, tools and approaches.

Investor confidence

Investors are more confident in trading with investment firms that adhere to the GIPS standards, especially in terms of fair representation and the ability to compete for highly profitable investment instruments all over the world.

GIPS Objectives

By creating GIPS standards, the investment industry benefited from an accepted set of practices that help in establishing the investment performance of different firms, irrespective of their jurisdiction. In order to foster better interaction between clients and their investment firms, the GIPS executive committee has the following objectives:

Encourage investment firms to self-regulate worldwide.

Promote the application of consistent and accurate data on investment performance.

Create the best industry practices for safeguarding investor interests and confidence, and promoting investment performance.

Push for globally accepted standards vis-à-vis full disclosure and fair representation.

Create a healthy investment environment for investors and investment firms by eliminating entry barriers.

While the GIPS standards do not exhaust all the asset classes, their dynamic evolution over time will strive to include more guidelines for investment performance, with an emphasis on risk and return for the investor.

According to the GIPS standards, investment firms must have a historical performance record to show for their effort. This means the following:

They must keep a record of no less than five years of investment performance records that meet the GIPS standards. For infant firms that have been in business for a shorter duration, they must present records since inception.

Firms must present their performance records annually, culminating in a decade of performance records.

Firms must disclose years of non-compliance to GIPS standards if they wish to link non-compliant records to their compliant records.

The GIPS executive committee has been working with different industry regulators to ensure compliance. In this regard, the regulators are expected to do the following:

Be on the lookout for misrepresentation, and firms that claim compliance falsely.

Encourage investment firms to self-regulate and comply with GIPS standards.

Encourage independent third parties to verify GIPS compliance.

All this must take place within the confines of the applicable laws and standards in the industry, and jurisdiction of the regulatory bodies.

GIPS Provisions

There are nine applicable provisions in the GIPS standards that cover recommendations and expectations that firms must adhere to in order to be considered GIPS compliant. They are industry best practices, and are as follows:

Fundamentals of compliance

The investment firm must be properly and clearly defined, making sure that prospective clients have complete information about the firm. The investment firm must also abide by all the laws applicable in their jurisdiction, along with regulations, and ensure it is not liable for misrepresentation.

Input data

There must be consistency in presenting input data, as this is important to determining performance and compliance with GIPS requirements. Investment periods beginning 1st January 2011 must have all portfolios valued as per GIPS valuation principles and fair value definition.

Calculation methods

For the sake of comparability, investment firms must apply uniform methods in calculating returns.

Composite construction

It is imperative that investment firms create useful composites to help in consistency, fair representation and comparability of performance for different investment firms.

Full disclosure

Under full disclosure, firms must strive to ensure they present correct and elaborate data that provides the client or audience the right context to make decisions on the performance of their portfolio, and the investment firm.

Reporting and presentation

All the information gathered must be presented according to the GIPS standards for reporting the performance of the investment firms. While there is no set of requirements currently that encompasses all the potential developments and situations, firms are encouraged to include all the relevant information, including those that are not defined by GIPS standards.

Real estate

Private equity

Separately managed account portfolios
In the case of real estate, private equity, and
separately managed account portfolios, all the
provisions applied in the first six above from
fundamentals of compliance to reporting and
presentation are applicable, unless otherwise
specified.

Practice Questions and Answers

1. An overconfidence bias makes it difficult for an
investment manager to conduct their business in an
ethical manner because it makes them
overestimate the moral implications of their:

A. Company
B. Personal behavior
C. Clients

The correct answer is B

Overconfidence bias is one of the biggest
challenges investors have to overcome in the
course of their business. Many people assume and
even pretend that they are professionals and
experts, and as a result, they hold themselves in a
higher ethical regard than everyone else. Because
of this kind of overconfidence, they overlook some
of the most important factors they should consider
when making investment decisions. As a result,
their decisions are not ethical.

2. Having researched on Schedule Dot Inc, Paul
has realized inconsistencies and is about to write
an unfavorable report about Schedule Dot Inc.
However, Paul's immediate supervisor is
concerned that this report will negatively affect the

relationship between their company and Schedule Dot Inc., one of their biggest investors, and requests him to exclude any adverse statements in his report. The following actions by Paul's supervisor are in violation of Standard I (B): Independence and Objectivity. Which of them is the most likely violation Paul's supervisor is about to impose?

A. Request Paul to state only facts about Schedule Dot. Inc

B. Instruct Paul to add Schedule Dot. Inc on their restricted list

C. Insist that Paul writes a favorable report for Schedule Dot. Inc

The correct answer is A

Standard I (B) clearly states that if a firm does not wish to provide harmful information about their client, they should include the client on their restricted list. In so doing, the firm will only be able to release accurate and factual information about their client.

3. Shirley is an account manager at Axe Capital. One of their clients, Tristan, sent Shirley an email, requesting her to purchase 3,000 shares in an IPO for Burt Corp's stock. Three weeks after Tristan's request, Shirley overcame the odds and prorated 5,000 shares of Burt Corp for their clients. Shirley honored Tristan's request of purchasing 3,000 shares, and purchased the remaining 2,000 shares for her husband. Which of the following best describes Shirley's position?

A. Shirley breached the standards by purchasing 2,000 shares for her husband, and only 3,000 for Tristan.

B. Shirley did not breach any standards by purchasing 2,000 shares for her husband and only 3,000 shares for Tristan.

C. Shirley maintained compliance by purchasing 3,000 shares for Tristan according to his request, but was only in breach of compliance when she purchased 2,000 shares for her husband.

The correct answer is A

In an IPO, the legal obligation of a member or candidate is to their clients. They must honor the clients and act fairly. They are barred from purchasing securities for their personal benefit. This stipulation cannot be overridden even by consent from the client. Given that the IPO was a hot issue, Shirley should have allocated the 5,000 shares to all their clients on a pro-rata basis.

4. Shoal Technologies is a research firm that hires the best analysts in the industry. Once hired, they offer the best training services, and enroll their analysts into financial courses to make sure they have the most competent and best analysts in the market. Shoal Technologies does not bar their analysts from using secondary research information or conducting their private research. One of their analysts takes advantage of this and relies on a research report prepared by Pinnacle Capital. What will happen if the analyst uses Pinnacle Capital's report?

A. The analyst is not in violation of any standards if they take precaution to ascertain the credibility of the research, and proceeds to use it in good faith.
B. The analyst violates Standard IV (A) Loyalty to employers because employees are prohibited from using the report from Pinnacle Capital.
C. The analyst is in violation of Standard I(C) Misrepresentation because they are depending on a report that was neither prepared by their clients nor themselves.

The correct answer is B

The analyst violates Standard IV-A Loyalty to employers because only secondary research is allowed. Secondary research refers to a report that is produced by one of their colleagues, within Shoal Technologies. The Pinnacle Capital report is a third-party research, whose use is in breach of Shoal Technology terms and conditions.

5. As an analyst, which information should you most likely disclose in order to avoid plagiarism in your work?
A. Sources of information from reports by other analysts and other publicly available information.
B. Summary reports by other analysts.
C. Information that is available in public.

The correct answer is A

Standard I (C): Misrepresentation stipulates that it is the analyst's duty to disclose all the sources of their information, even if the information is in the public domain. They must also disclose whether they are using summary notes or reports that were prepared by someone other than themselves.

6. A company that is fully compliant with the GIPS standards is not expected to:

A. Place a competitive bid against other GIPS compliant firms.

B. Offer assurances to their potential clients that their historical track record gives a true, complete, and fair representation of their company.

C. Ignore the need to carry out deep research and due diligence on behalf of their investors.

The correct answer is C

According to GIPS standards, firms that are compliant can participate in global financial markets and place competitive bids against other firms. The firms can also assure their clients that their historical track records reported are a true and fair representation of their position.

The GIPS standards, however, do not excuse the firm from ignoring their due diligence obligations to their investors.

7. Sean Paul, CFA is a research analyst at one of the top brokerage firms in the country. Sean's wife Melinda, CFA is also a research analyst in a different brokerage firm. Sean is working from home one morning, and receives a call from one of the investment bankers. The investment banker informs Sean that one of the largest companies in his portfolio is about to be taken over at a 47% premium against the prevailing market rate. While this information is not in the public domain yet,

Melinda overhears the conversation and proceeds to purchase the stock for her clients. Who among the three most likely violated Standard II (A): Material Non-Public Information?

A. Sean and Melinda
B. All of them
C. Sean and his investment banker

The correct answer is B

They all violated Standard II (A) in the following manner:

Sean was at fault because he had the chance to prevent the transfer and misuse of material, non-public information, but he did not, and instead acted on it.

The investment banker had an obligation to keep the information to himself as it was not released to the public yet, but he chose not to.

Melinda acted on material, non-public information.

8. A portfolio manager tells one of their potential clients that they are unable to guarantee the client will earn 15% on equities in the current financial year, but instead, they can provide a range in which they expect the client's returns to fall. The portfolio manager proceeds to relate that he is popular with his clients because for the last 7 years, his range is always right. He arrives at the range by implementing professionally accredited reports, economic forecasts, and financial models. Based on the standards of the CFA Institute, the portfolio manager:

A. Is in violation of Standard I (C): Misrepresentation

B. Is in violation of Standard III (D): Performance Presentation

C. Is not in violation of any standard

The correct answer is A

By providing the potential client a range, the portfolio manager is adjudged to be in violation of Standard I (C): Misrepresentation. Portfolio managers are barred from assuring clients specific returns, including a range of returns. Investments carry risk, which make the returns unpredictable. Therefore, by giving a range of returns, the manager has misled the investors.

9. Which of the following is not the most likely feature of GIPS?

A. The investment firm must include all the discretionary portfolios that pay fees in composites, according to a specific investment objective or strategy

B. Once the firm has presented five years of their compliance history, they must add annual performance every subsequent year up to a maximum period of ten years.

C. The investment management firm is expected to define the entity which claims compliance

The correct answer is B

Initially, an investment firm is expected to present at least five years proof of their compliance. After that, they are expected to present their performance annually for a period of at least 10 years.

10. Carlton has been a financial analyst with Bert Securities for seven years. While at Bert, his portfolio included Mac Corp, and he had built an elaborate financial model, complete with reports and credible assumptions. Carlton got a new job with a different company, and in his new position, he was once again tasked with analyzing Mac Corp. Carlton went ahead and created a better financial model, improving on all the specifications, reporting and assumptions he used at Bert Securities. Has Carlton violated any standards of the CFA Institute?

A. Carlton is in violation of Standard V(C): Record Retention because he recreated supporting records for Mac Corp.

B. Yes. Carlton is in violation of Record Retention and Misrepresentation because he recreated the Mac Corp model.

C. No. Carlton has fully complied with the Code and Standards of the CFA Institute

The correct answer is C

Carlton has not violated any standards and codes as specified by the CFA Institute. He built a new model, and only recreated the supporting records by obtaining information directly from Mac Corp.

11. In line with the CFA Institute standards of professional conduct, which of the following information is a firm not expected to most likely disclose to their clients?

A. Any extra compensation that a member of the firm earns if in their free time, they tutor candidate on how to prepare for the CFA exam.
B. Disclosure about the firm's personal holdings
C. Information about referral fees

The correct answer is A

In Standard VI (A): Disclosure of Conflicts, members are required to fully disclose any information or matter that might impair their ability to objectively and independently exercise their duty and obligation to their employer, clients or potential clients.

In the scenario above, the employee clearly offers tutorial services in their spare time. It is highly unlikely that this will affect their ability to carry out their mandate. However, the employee should ensure the employer is duly informed.

12. Following the requirements of Standard II (A): Material Non-Public Information, what is expected of a CFA member if they come across information that they believe is material?
A. Ensure the information is publicly disseminated
B. Use the information to influence their clients' current investment portfolio.
C. Protect the information from anyone who might have access to it or act on it.

The correct answer is A

If any candidate or member comes across material information, they are expected to take the necessary action to ensure it is disseminated for public consumption.

13. Quinton has been a financial analyst for Green Core Inc for 15 years. Blue Tech recently acquired his services. Upon starting his contract at Blue Tech, Quinton realizes that he can contact his former clients and invite them to move with him to Blue Tech. He knows them well, and they have mutual trust and confidence in him, having handled their portfolios in the past. Which is the most likely infringement Quinton will be guilty of if he goes ahead with this action?

A. Quinton will not have violated Standard IV (A): Loyalty. This is because the question does not indicate that Quinton signed any non-compete clause with Green Core Inc. Therefore, Quinton can use the information he has in his memory.

B. Quinton will violate Standard IV (A): Loyalty if he uses the previous client list, having obtained it from Green Core Inc with permission, and contacts the clients.

C. Quinton will violate Standard IV (A): Loyalty because he has not signed a non-compete clause with Green Core Inc. but proceeds to contact the former clients.

The correct answer is A

According to Standard IV (A), knowledge of the names of former clients is not considered confidential information. Because of this reason, the employee can use this information to benefit their new employer just in the same way that the new employer is benefitting from the employee's expertise, skills and experience gained in the former place of employment. Without a non-compete clause, employees can contact their former clients when they move to a new firm.

14. You are one of the directors of Stealth Financial Advisors. You are sent to represent the company in brief meetings across different states in the country. Most of your company's clients will be present in these meetings, since the brief meetings will also be used to launch the company's Silver Jubilee celebrations.

As you go through your presentation, you carefully reference all the information you presented, and give a detailed report to back your presentation. At the end of your presentation, you share the report only with the clients who request a copy, instead of making the report available to all the clients in attendance. In so doing, you have:

A. Violated Standard III (D) Performance Presentation

B. Violated Standard III (B) Fair Dealing

C. Did not violate any of the CFA standards

The correct answer is C

Standard III (D) Performance Presentation stipulates that if your performance presentation is brief, you must only make it available to your current clients and potential clients upon their request. In due diligence, your presentation must also reference the brief nature of the presentation.

15. Misleading practices in the company can be least likely resolved by GIPS standards because of:

A. Adjustments to financial statements by analysts

B. Different time intervals

C. Bias in the form of survivorship

The correct answer is A

GIPS standards can be used to resolve misleading practices in the company, including, but not necessarily limited to the following:

Different time intervals

Bias in the form of survivorship

The presence of representative accounts

16. You are an account manager, handling individual accounts for your investment firm, one of which belongs to your uncle. Over the weekend you meet one of your friends at a restaurant for lunch and notice LG Electronics directors in a discussion in the next booth. Your friend mentions that LG Electronics has recently brought in a new CEO in line with a management shake-up to streamline their production line.

When you get to the office on Monday morning, you realize the price of LG Electronics has gone up by $2.30 and decide to buy 10,000 shares for your uncle's account. Which of these standards will you be least likely to have violated?

A. Standard II (A): Material Non-Public Information

B. Standard IV (B): Priority of Transactions

C. Standard V (A): Diligence and Reasonable Basis

The correct answer is A

The fact that you used your friend's opinion, which is not backed by any factual knowledge, does not constitute material information.

You were, however, in violation of Standard VI (B): Priority of Transactions because you made a conscious decision to purchase stocks only for your uncle's account, in the process giving that account an unfair advantage over all the other client accounts in your care.

You also violated Standard V (A): Diligence and Reasonable Basis because you went ahead and purchased LG Electronics shares out of speculation without conducting sufficient research to understand the reason behind the price change.

17. Clara is a portfolio manager at Techtronic Investments. Recently, her employer issued a lot of shares in an IPO for a company that Clara has been bullish about. Clara got carried away by the possibility of earning her clients amazing return on their investment, and as a result, went ahead and distributed the shares equally in all the accounts she was managing. It happens that some of these accounts are held by her family members. Clara was most likely guilty of:

A. Standard III (A) Loyalty, Prudence and Care
B. Standard III (C): Suitability
C. Clara did not breach any standards in her actions

The correct answer is B

Before she allocated the shares to the accounts she was managing, Clara did not take time to ascertain the suitability of the investment, beyond her deep bullish feelings towards the stock. As a result, she breached Standard III (C) Suitability because every account is held under specific risk tolerance levels and investor objectives.

18. Jane and Parker are very good friends. Jane is an investment banker. She exclusively engages Parker through his brokerage firm, to make investment transactions for her clients. She prefers dealing with Parker over all the other brokers in the market because he offers the best services, though he charges a reasonable premium for his services, which Jane feels is worth the effort. Of the statements below that describe Jane, which is the least inaccurate?

A. Jane is not violating any standard.

B. Jane violates Standard III (A): Loyalty, Prudence, and Care.

C. Jane violates Standard III (B): Fair Dealing

The correct answer is A

Regardless of what Parker is charging, Jane is within her rights to prefer dealing with Parker as her broker. The premiums Parker is charging for his brokerage services are also justified in the provision of excellent services, better than everyone else in the market.

19. Considering the key sections of the GIPS standards, which of the statements below are the least likely incorrect?

A. Section 3: Composite Construction – a composite return refers to the performance asset-weighted average for all portfolios in a composite.

B. Section 4: Disclosures – companies are duly expected to indicate negative assurance disclosures

C. Section 5: Presentation and Reporting – companies are barred from including information that does not meet the GIPS standards in presentations that are GIPS compliant.

The correct answer is C

Section 5 allows companies to include information that does not meet the GIPS standards in their GIPS compliant presentation, only when they feel it is appropriate.

20. In light of Standard III (C) Preservation of Confidentiality, CFA members are required to uphold the confidentiality of information that is communicated to them by:

A. Potential and current clients only

B. Potential, current, and former clients.

C. Former and current clients only.

The correct answer is B

According to Standard III (E), members are expected to uphold the integrity and confidentiality of any information that is shared with them by any of their clients, irrespective of whether they are current, former or potential clients.

21. Patricia is an account manager for Shapely Advisory. She also manages a trust fund account for Pliers Trust. Recently, Pliers Trust offered Patricia $100,000 as a cash gift if she could succeed in earning their trust a 19% return. What is the best course of action for Patricia?

A. Patricia should accept Pliers Trust's offer, and work towards meeting their agreed target without compromising the rest of her clients, and conduct herself objectively.

B. Patricia should immediately write to Shapely Advisory management, indicating that Pliers Trust is offering her a $100,000 cash gift.

C. Patricia should reject Pliers Trust's offer so there is no conflict of interest with Shapely Advisory.

The correct answer is B

In Standard IV (B): Additional Compensation Arrangements, Patricia is expected to disclose, in writing, any compensation she expects or proposes from any client, other than the benefits and compensation she gets from Shapely Advisory.

22. Which of the following activities is least likely to be a violation of Standard VII (B): Reference to CFA Institute, the CFA Designation and the CFA Program?

A. A Level II candidate who refers to themselves as CFA, I

B. A Level III candidate who is waiting for their results, referring to themselves as CFA, expected 2019.

C. An investment manager who claims that their successful completion of the CFA course is responsible for improving their portfolio management ability.

The correct answer is C

Statement A and B are in violation of Standard VII (B).

Chapter 2: Quantitative Methods

In this section, you will learn about quantitative techniques and concepts that you will use in financial analysis to help in decision making.

Time Value of Money

Time value of money deals with investment relationships around the value of cash flows at different points in time. What you can do with $1,000 today might not be the same as what you can do with the $1,000 ten years from now. To make up for this, interest is charged or discounts applied.

An interest rate, often denoted by r, is the rate of return you expect from a given investment over a period of time. Interest rates can be one of the following in any investment:

Required rate of return on investment

Discount rate

Opportunity cost – the cost in terms of the best foregone alternative

In economic terms, interest rates are determined by the forces of demand and supply. In the case of investors, interest is earned as a factor of compensation for assuming risk. Hence, the following formula applies:

r = real risk-free interest rate + inflation premium + liquidity premium + default risk premium + maturity premium

What do these terms mean?

Real risk-free interest rate – Interest rate over one period for a risk-free security without expecting inflation.

Inflation premium – this is investor compensation for anticipated inflation until the debt facility matures.

Liquidity premium – compensating an investor for taking on risk, and the possibility of loss on the par value of the investment, if it is converted to cash.

Default risk premium – investor compensation in light of the fact that the borrower might fail to honor their agreement.

Maturity premium – investor compensation in light of market sensitivity to the debt value

Your initial investment is represented by the present value (PV). It earns interest (r) during its lifetime, and at maturity, it has a future value (FV) at the end of a given period of time (N). The future value of a single cash flow can therefore be represented by the following equation:

$FV_N = PV(1+r)$

Investing $1,000 in a product that earns you 5% a year, the future value of your investment at the end of the first year will be as follows:

$FV = \$1000(1+0.05) = \$1050$

If you keep the investment for two years, the money in your account at the beginning of the second year will be $1,050, which becomes the present value. At the end of the second year, your account should have:

$= \$1050(1+0.05) = \$1102.5$

As your investment grows, you keep earning interest on interest. This is referred to as compounding. The formula for compounding interest over several investment periods is as follows:

$FV_N = PV(1+r)^N$

In our investment above after two years, the future value of the investment would be:

$= \$1000(1+0.05)^2 = \$1102.5$

Some investments earn interest several times a year, probably at the end of each month. If your bank offers 8% a year as interest compounded on a monthly basis, basically each month you are getting 8%/12 months, which is 0.67%. In such investments, the formula for the future value changes to:

$FV_N = PV(1+r_s/m)^{mN}$

In this equation, m represents the number of compounding periods in that trading year, and N represents the number of years.

If you invest $1000 earning you 8% quarterly over two years, at the point of maturity your investment will have grown as follows:

$FV_N = PV(1+r_s/m)^{mN}$
$= 1000(1+0.08/4)^{4(2)}$
$= 1000(1.02)^8$
$= 1,171.66$

Discounted Cash Flow Applications

Projects that have unique payoffs can be compared through the internal rate of return (IRR) and net present value (NPV). This can help the company determine the best project to invest their resources. The formula for NPV is as follows

$$NPV = \sum C_t(1+r)^t$$

C_t refers to the cash flow at a given point in time, t. r refers to the discount rate.

NPV is the aggregate of all the cash inflows and outflows, discounted at a specific rate of return to determine the value of the project at the present moment. A positive result indicates a sound project, while a negative result indicates an unfavorable, loss-making projection. On the same note, of two or more projects, the higher NPV indicates a better investment.

The IRR refers to a return rate on a project which results in zero NPV. In whichever problem you are solving, a higher value often indicates the better option. You also need to learn about the following types of return:

Holding period return (HPR)

This refers to the project's return over its lifetime. It is calculated by the following formula:

HPR = (Closing value – Opening value + Income)/ Opening value

Money-weighted rate of return (MWRR)

This refers to a specific portfolio's IRR. It is the discount rate where the present value of cash inflows is equal to the present value of cash outflows.

Time-weighted rate of return (TWRR)

This refers to the geometric average for each year's investment HPR.

Returns on fixed income securities can be calculated in several ways. One common method is the holding period yield, which is calculated using the HPR formula.

Statistical Concepts and Market Returns

When dealing with statistical concepts and market returns, you need to learn about the arithmetic mean, weighted mean, geometric mean and the harmonic mean. These calculations will be the core of your work going forward.

Other than the mean averages, you must also learn how to find the variance of a given set of numbers. Variance refers to the average of squared deviations from the norm. After finding the variance, you square it to find the standard deviation.

Mean absolute deviation is arrived at by measuring the absolute deviation values from the mean for a given set of values.

The Sharpe ratio determines a portfolio's returns after adjusting for risk. A high value indicates the prospect of high returns for every risk exposure. The formula is as follows:

Sharpe ratio = (Portfolio return – Risk-free rate of return)/ standard deviation of the portfolio returns

When studying different sets of data, you can represent them according to the distribution, hence skewness or kurtosis. Kurtosis represents how data is distributed from the normal distribution.

Mesokurtic distribution refers to data that almost

looks like the normal distribution pattern.

Leptokurtic distribution refers to data that is closely grouped around the average. Platykurtic distribution refers to data that is distributed widely.

Probability

Probability is about chances of an event or multiple events occurring, given the chance of a certain event occurring. The normal probability formula follows the multiplication rule, and is shown as follows:

$P(AB) = P(A|B) P(B)$

This means that the joint probability that event A and B happen ($P(AB)$), depends on the probability of event A happening, assuming that event B also happens ($P(A|B)$), multiplied by the probability of event B happening ($P(B)$)

The probability that event A or B happen can be represented as follows:

$P (A \text{ or } B) = P(A) + P(B) - P(AB)$

Correlation and covariance are two important concepts that you must remind yourself about. Correlation is the covariance ratio between two variables, and their standard deviations.

Covariance, on the other hand, refers to the degree of synchrony between two variables.

The covariance of two portfolio assets (a and b) can be represented by the formula below:

$\sigma Ra,Rb = \sum P(Ra)[Ra - E(Ra)][Rb - E(Rb)]$

When solving questions that involve variance and standard deviations, especially in correlation, you must be very keen on the data provided. Portfolio risk can be presented as a variance or standard deviation. Whichever the case, remember that variance is the square of standard deviation.

From the answer you get, the following rules apply for the correlation values:

-1 – the assets are moving in opposite directions

0 – there is no relationship between the assets

1 – the assets are moving in the same direction

Probability Distribution

You have a discrete uniform random variable if all the events have the same probability of happening, as in the case of rolling a die. In the case of a Bernoulli random variable, you can only have two outcomes, all of which are independent of one another, as in the case of a coin toss.

The Bernoulli effect can be represented by a Bernoulli tree, where the final outcome is as a result of successful repetitions of Bernoulli events. The easiest way to detect errors in your calculations when using a Bernoulli tree is that at any given point, the total probability must always be 100%. If you have anything to the contrary, your calculations must be wrong.

Roy's Safety-First Ratio is another method you can use to monitor exposure to risks. According to this principle, the best or optimal portfolio should be one where there is a lower probability of returning yields lower than the acceptable threshold, which is referred to as a shortfall risk.

The formula for the safety-first ratio is represented as follows:

(Expected returns – Threshold returns)/ Standard deviation

Sampling and Estimation

Statistics relies on data samples to determine information about a specific data set. According to the central limit theorem, any data sample must have a variance and mean that is as close to the variance and mean of the population under representation as the study sample grows in size. The Student's T-Distribution is one of the best methods of determining the probability distribution of a given set of data. It is an appropriate method especially where you don't have the variance of the population. The formula is as follows:

(Sample mean – Population mean)/ (Standard deviation/Square root of the sample size)

Confidence intervals represent the value range wherein you can find the population parameters. Confidence intervals consider confidence and the range of values in such a way that there is lower confidence when dealing with a smaller value set.

Hypothesis Testing

This is a process by which you determine whether a specific data point in your distribution is significant. One-tailed tests determine the probability of change in one direction. Two-tailed tests determine the probability of positive and negative directional changes. These tests help to determine whether you should accept or refute the hypothesis presented.

The formula for testing hypothesis is as follows:

(Sample statistic – Hypothesis value) / Standard error for the sample statistic

When testing a hypothesis, you can encounter the following errors:

Type 1 error – happens when the hypothesis is a true null, but you reject it.

Type 2 error – happens when the hypothesis is a false null, but you accept it.

P-values are also important in hypothesis testing. If the level of significance is greater than your P-value, you can reject the null hypothesis.

The Z-test gives us a correct hypothesis for a normal distribution, and can be represented by the following formula:

Z -statistic = (Sample mean – Hypothesized population mean) / (Standard deviation of the population / Square root of the sample size)

Statistical tests can be classified in the following groups:

Parametric tests – All parameters follow a unique distribution pattern.

Non-parametric tests – No assumptions are made about the distribution pattern.

Technical Analysis

Technical analysis refers to a situation where volume and price data about a given stock is used to determine its value. In technical analysis, you should learn how to read trends. Trends indicate the direction of movement of a given security over a period of time. Trends are a comparative tool for identifying the difference between demand and supply.

Support and resistance levels are price points where activities in the market conspire to ensure the security does not fall above or below a given point. Further to this, the principle of change in polarity applies to support and resistance. This means that if the security breaches the set level, it becomes the opposite. What this means is that if the security breaches the resistance level, the new price point becomes its support point.

Stock charts represent different patterns in technical analysis, which can be used to estimate the future price movements. A reversal pattern is an indication that the trend might regress. A head and shoulders pattern is a sign of the end of an upward trend. A continuation pattern signifies a trend that might persist even after a pause.

The following are some of the indicators that can be used in technical analysis to determine the prospective changes in the future for security prices:

Sentiment indicators

These are polls carried out to determine investor perception of the equity market at a given point in time.

Momentum oscillators

The values are arrived at from the difference between the previous price at a given date in the past, and the most recent price point for a security.

If the value changes from positive to negative, there is a chance of trend reversal.

It is calculated by the following formula:

(Most recent closing price – Closing price at a given date in the past) x 100

Price-based indicators

The future price of a security is derived from studying information about the past prices and the present price. One of the techniques used is the moving averages.

Fund flow indicators

These indicators monitor rising and declining stocks by measuring the amount of money flowing in or out of these counters to determine behavior. Any values more than 1 represent a high volume of stocks that are declining. Values lower than 1 represent more investment activity in the rising stocks.

When forecasting the behavior of securities in the market, you will also need to look at cycles. Trade cycles are movement patterns in the market that take place over a given time. Some cycles can happen in the course of a single trading day several times, while others can take years to recur.

Practice Questions and Answers

1. Which of the following charts, when drawn on a grid, has the O column in alternation with the X column, but most likely does not have the column representing volume or time?

A. Candlestick chart

B. Bar chart

C. Point and figure chart

The correct answer is C

You need a graph paper to draw a point and figure chart. The X column and O column alternate, but the graph does not have a volume or time representation.

2. You are an analyst and you need to present some stocks to your supervisor after rating them as outperform, neutral, and underperform. What is the best scale to represent this data?

A. Interval scale

B. Ordinal scale

C. Ratio scale

The correct answer is B

According to the specifications, you need to rate the stocks based on their expected performance in the future, not the performance differences between the asset classes, hence an ordinal scale would be the best option.

3. When you are analyzing mutually exclusive projects, why shouldn't you choose the IRR rule over NPV?

A. When using the IRR ranking, you assume the possibility of reinvestment at the opportunity cost of capital, which is not relevant economically, hence less realistic.

B. Discount rates and interest rates from external factors influence NPV rankings.

C. NPV uses more conservative reinvestment rates, making it a relevant option.

The correct answer is B

The NPV rule is hugely dependent on the external market forces to determine the discount rate. This is because of the expectation of reinvestment at the opportunity cost of capital. When using IRR, the assumption is that any cash flows will be reinvested in the project, and for that reason the rankings are not influenced by external discounts or interest rates.

4. In the last 24 months, you have obtained the following information concerning the return on an investment:

Mean return = 15%

Standard deviation of returns = 9%

Assuming a 4% risk-free rate, what is the closest figure to the Sharpe ratio for this particular investment?

A. 1.02

B. 1.22

C. 0.33

The correct answer is B

The Sharpe ratio is calculated as follows:

$(0.15 - 0.04)/0.09 = 1.22$

5. An analyst estimates that there is a 25% probability that the stock market will rise in value in the next year. Which is the closest odd that you can provide against the value of the market rising?

A. 3 to 1

B. 1 to 3

C. 1 to 5

The correct answer is A

In probabilistic computations, odds stacked against an event happening are computed as follows:

= P (event not happening) to P (event happening)

= (1 – 25%) to (25%)

= 75% to 25%

= 3 to 1

6. Assuming a normal random variable, 67% of all the outcomes will fall within which of the following possibilities?

A. Two standard deviations of the mean

B. One standard deviation of the mean

C. Three standard deviations of the mean

The correct answer is B

In a normal random variable, approximately 67% of all the outcomes will be found within a single standard deviation of the mean.

7. The following information is available about the return distribution for two unique portfolios.

Portfolio X – 2.4 Kurtosis and – 3.6 Skewness

Portfolio Y – 1.2 Kurtosis and + 4.1 Skewness

What is the most likely correct statement that describes the portfolios?

A. More than half of the deviations from the mean in Portfolio Z are negative

B. The distribution in Portfolio X has a few large gains against a lot of small losses.

C. Portfolio X features a greater peak than a normal distribution

The correct answer is A

From analysis, we can see that Portfolio Z is positively skewed. This can be attributed to very few large gains against many small losses. The right side of this portfolio has a longer tail than the left side.

In case a distribution has a greater mean than the median and is positively skewed, most of its deviations from the mean will be negative, and fewer than half of the deviations will be positive.

8. An investment fund had the following information for the year ended 31st December, 2018:

Fund market value on 1st January 2018 of $70 million

18% holding period return between 1st January and 30th June

The fund had a $35 million fund injection at the beginning of July 2018

On 31st December, 2018 the dividends worth $8 million were released into the fund

The market value of the fund at the end of 2018 was $134 million, including the dividends.

Determine the closest time weighted return for the investment fund.

A. 22.21%

B. 34.46%

C. 12.93%

The correct answer is B

We will factor in two periods, 1st January to 30th June, and 1st July to 31st December 2018.

Period 1: 1st January – 30th June

Opening market value = $70 million

Holding period return = 18%

Closing market value = (1.18 * 70 million) = $82.6 million

Period 2: 1st July – 31st December, 2018

Added investment into the fund = $35 million

Opening market value = ($82.5 million + $35 million) = $117.6 million

Holding period return = (134 - 117.6) / 117.6 = 13.95%

The average time weighted rate of return = (1.18 *1.1395) = 34.46%

9. Which among the following is the most possible scenario in a portfolio?

A. Many investors favor a higher SF ratio portfolio because of its low likelihood of delivering yields lower than the threshold level.

B. Many investors favor a lower SF ratio portfolio because of its high likelihood of delivering yields higher than the threshold level

C. Many investors favor a higher SF ratio portfolio because of its low likelihood of delivering yields higher than the threshold level.

The correct answer is A

A high SF ratio portfolio is considered to have a very low risk of delivering yields below the threshold level, hence many investors prefer such a portfolio.

10. Given the following standard deviations and sample sizes for a random variable, which of the options has a high probability of delivering the smallest confidence?

Standard deviation   Sample Size

A. Greater	Greater
B. Greater	Lower
C. Lower	Greater

The correct answer is C

In a random variable distribution, you need a large sample size to derive a low standard deviation. As a result, this is the only option that can deliver a narrow confidence interval.

11. You are presented with a single normal distribution population, and asked to test the variance of the distribution. Which is the most probable test you will use?

A. Chi-square test

B. F-test

C. T-test

The correct answer is A

In a single normal distribution population, the best test to determine the variance is a Chi-square test. An F-test is best applied when you need to determine the variance equality between two population distributions. A T-test is used to carry out tests on the mean.

12. Given a sample distribution, how would you measure the efficiency of an unbiased estimator?

A. Median value

B. Variance

C. Sample size

The correct answer is B

Variance is used to determine the efficiency of an unbiased estimator. In case no other unbiased estimator is available of similar characteristics and parameters and a smaller variance, the unbiased estimator in question is deemed efficient.

13. The following statements describe covariance and correlation properties. Which of the statements is the most correct?

A. Correlation is only concerned with linear relationships between variables.

B. If the correlation between two variables A and B is greater than zero, the variables are said to be in perfect positive linear correlation.

C. The more securities are added into a portfolio, the covariance value diminishes, holding all factors constant.

The correct answer is A

Correlation indeed deals with linear relationships. In the other statements, variables A and B can only be said to be in perfect positive linear correlation if the correlation between them is greater than 1.

As you increase the number of securities held in a portfolio, the value of covariance increases too, holding all other factors constant.

14. What happens when you increase the frequency of compounding at a predetermined annual interest rate?

A. The present and future value of the amount decrease.

B. The present and future value of the amount increase.

C. The present value of the amount decreases, but the future value increases

The correct answer is C

The effective annual rate increases when you increase the frequency of compounding. Based on this assertion, therefore, the present value of the amount will reduce while the future value will increase.

15. Nine students are invited to participate in a math contest. Only the top three students in the contest will be awarded. What is the closest number of ways that the top three awards will be distributed?

A. 27

B. 210

C. 504

The correct answer is C

The most important factor in this estimation is the order in which the top three students will perform in the contest. The awards will be given according to the order of performance. Because of this reason, therefore, the following permutations formula applies:

$9P3 = 9! / (9 - 3)! = 504$

16. Determine the standard deviation for five students who scored the following results in a recent examination: 70%, 85%, 90%, 62%, and 55%

A. 14.83%

B. 16.64%

C. 13.59%

The correct answer is C

The mean score

$= (70 + 85 + 90 + 62 + 55) / 5 = 72.4\%$

Standard deviation

$= \{[(70 - 72.4)2 + (85 - 72.4) 2 + (90 - 72.4) 2 + (62 - 72.4) 2 + (55 - 72.4) 2]5\} / (5 - 1)$

$= (5.76 + 158.76 + 309.76 + 108.16 + 302.76) 5$

$= (885.2) 5 / 4$

$= 13.59\%$

17. Determine the closest money market yield for a T-bill that has a $2,000 face value, which is currently valued at $1850, with 100 days remaining until maturity.

A. 27.34%

B. 29.20%

C. 24.28%

The correct answer is B

The HPY

$= [(2,000 - 1850) / 1850] \times 100 = 8.11\%$

Money market yield

$= HPY \times 360/t$

$= 8.11\% \times 3.6$

$= 29.20\%$

18. You are requested to rate different stocks in the market based on their performance, as either neutral, outperforming, or under-performing. Which kind of scale will you use to measure this data?

A. Ratio scale

B. Ordinal scale

C. Interval scale

The correct answer is B

The stocks mentioned above are rated according to the expected performance in the future. There is no information in the classifications about the performance difference between the different stocks, so an ordinal scale will be the best option.

19. While observing information in a data set, you realize that the information you are provided does not share similarities in value. What would be your conclusion regarding the geometric mean, harmonic mean and arithmetic mean of the data set?

A. Geometric mean is greater than the arithmetic mean, which is greater than the harmonic mean
B. Arithmetic mean is greater than the harmonic mean, which is greater than the geometric mean
C. Arithmetic mean is greater than the geometric mean, which is greater than the harmonic mean

The correct answer is C

In a data set whose data do not share any similarities in value, the harmonic mean is usually smaller than the geometric mean, which is smaller than the arithmetic mean.

20. The following characteristics are applicable to estimators. Which of the characteristics is the most unlikely for an estimator?

A. Continuity
B. Consistency
C. Efficiency

The correct answer is A

A desirable estimator should be consistent, efficient, and unbiased.

21. You are working with a two-tailed hypothesis test which has a 0.5 p-value. If the level of

significance is 6%, what is the least unlikely null
hypothesis for this test?
A. Accept
B. Reject
C. Not rejected
The correct answer is B
The p-value represents the lowest possible
significance level where you can reject the null
hypothesis. Given that the significance level is 6%,
the null hypothesis is rejected because the p-value
for this test (5%) is less than the significance level.
In a hypothesis test, the treatment for a null
hypothesis is to reject or not reject. It can never be
accepted.
Chapter 3: Economics
The study of economics will cover microeconomics
(the economic decisions of individual units) and
macroeconomics (decisions concerning
aggregates, like national income and output). In
microeconomics, economic units are classified
under consumers and firms, based on the need to
meet consumer demand with supply from the firms.
While consumers strive to maximize utility value,
firms look forward to maximizing their profit earning
capacity.
Demand and Supply Analysis
Consumers follow the law of demand, hence
purchasing less of an item if the price rises, and
more if the price falls. There are other variables
other than prices that determine the consumers'
willingness to purchase. Therefore, the quantity of

an item's demand will always be a function of its price, the individual's income, and the price of another item (substitutes and complements), giving us the equation below:

Q=f(Px, I, Py)

Q – quantity demanded of product X

Px – price of product X

Py –price of product y

I – consumer income

From time to time you will need to determine the sensitivity of quantity supplied and demanded in the market, in relation to different variables that affect them. This is the concept of elasticity of supply and demand. Elasticity is a measure of sensitivity of different variables in relation to others, and is measured in percentages.

Inelasticity is a situation where the magnitude of the elasticity coefficient is less than one. If it is greater than one, you have an elastic coefficient.

Remember that elasticity measures the sensitivity of one variable against another.

Income elasticity of demand is a measure of the percentage change in quantity demanded in relation to the percentage change in income.

The formula for elasticity is E = % change in Quantity divided by the % change in Price.

Concerning income elasticity, there are two different types of goods. For normal goods, the positive income elasticity is more than zero, which is a sign that there is a higher demand for them as the consumer's income increases. For inferior goods, the elasticity value is less than zero, which means the demand for them decreases as consumer income increases.

Some goods, like substitutes and complementary goods, share cross-price elasticity. This means that an increase in the price of one good results in higher demand for the other. This happens a lot for competing product brands, because the consumer will only need one of them. Complementary goods have negative cross price elasticity. If the price of one of the goods rises, the demand for its complements falls because consumers will always buy them together.

According to the law of diminishing returns, the marginal return from increasing input decreases when this happens. Take the example of a hungry adult. Two or three cookies will satisfy you and make you feel happier. However, if you keep eating more, you soon feel guilty.

The concept of economies of scale arises when the average cost of production reduces as a result of a higher production volume. We experience this so many times when shopping, because it is cheaper to buy some goods in bulk than to buy fewer items.

Market Structures and the Firm

The following are the main market structures:

Monopoly – one firm is in complete control of the entire market. Their position allows them to set prices and desired quantity of goods produced. This market has very many entry barriers, making it difficult for competitors to join.

Oligopoly – production is controlled by several firms in the market. The controlling firms in the market determine the price points, in order to maximize their profits. The barriers to entry are high, keeping new entrants at bay.

Perfect competition – the market features many firms, selling similar goods to consumers. Due to the similarity, it is impossible for a single firm to outgrow the competition to the point of controlling the market.

Monopolistic competition – this market features several firms who compete in the level of differentiation of their products. Differentiation allows some firms to gain more profit, but they cannot maintain the profit level in the long run.

Firms participating in either of these markets have only three profit outcomes. In the long run, there is no economic profit in a perfect competition. New firms are attracted by the prospect of profits, flooding the market with supply to the point where the marginal revenue from increased production is equal to the marginal cost of production ($MC = MR$).

In monopolistic competition, while the allure of profits attracts new entrants, the existing firms can still hold their fort through differentiation, giving them an edge over the competition. In an oligopoly, firms realize profits in the long term, but no single firm can earn sufficient profit to control the market. This is because competitors keep changing their operation strategies. Monopolies are the only markets where firms earn profits in the long run. From the revenue earned, monopolists strengthen their hold on the market by making the barriers to entry more stringent.

In terms of pricing strategies, firms operating in a perfect competition are price takers, and depend on the supply and demand curve to determine the optimal price. Monopolistic competitors control their prices through differentiation. Prices in oligopolies depend on the nature of competition. While it might be possible for some firms to influence the prices, none can exert complete control over them. Monopolies, on the other hand, create their own prices. However, they must also keep them reasonable enough to discourage new entrants.

Aggregate Output, Prices and Economic Growth

A country's measure of economic activity is referred to as the gross domestic product, GDP. This is the aggregate income of the government, and all firms and households in the country. Thus, GDP can be calculated as follows:

Income function: GDP = Total National Income + Sales Tax + Depreciation + Net Foreign Factor Income

Expenditure function: GDP = Consumer Expenditure + Investments + Government spending + Exports – Imports

GDP can be constructed as nominal GDP or real GDP. Nominal GDP is arrived at after adjusting for inflation. Real GDP is arrived at from the raw values. Inflation in nominal GDP is used to determine the present or future value of the GDP, hence referred to as a GDP deflator, with the following formula:

GDP Deflator = (Nominal GDP/ Real GDP) * 100

Estimated GDP growth can be classified into capital, labor, and technology. Labor productivity is arrived at in the following formula:

Labor productivity = (Real GDP/ Aggregate Man Hours)

Increasing labor productivity implies that the economy can achieve so much more without increasing the labor hours. From this understanding, improving operating technology can help increase the productivity of the workforce.

Business Cycles

A business cycle refers to the economy's growth pattern over a given period of time. A normal economy undergoes periods of growth and decline over time, with periods of recession and expansion in between. A business cycle has the following phases:

Peak – growth is halted by pressure from inflation on wages and prices

Contraction – the economy is slowing down, unemployment is on the rise, and prices fall.

Trough – the economy is on its knees.

Expansion – the economy is growing, there is pressure on prices, and the level of unemployment declines.

Business cycles can be explained in the following models:

Money model approach – business cycles are driven by the desire for money, and the fluctuations cause inflation.

New classical school of thought – business cycles are driven by buyers and sellers. The aggregate of buy/sell decisions eventually determine the performance of the economy.

Neoclassical school of thought – market equilibrium is arrived at automatically, unless under influence by the government.

Monetary/ Keynesian approach – in a recession, governments must apply fiscal policies to intervene and restore the economy to normalcy.

It is important to have proper working knowledge of inflation to make accurate economic analysis. The immediate result of inflation is diminishing purchasing power of consumers, culminating in a lethargic economy.

Monetary and Fiscal Policy

Fiscal policy is about the decisions made by the government about taxation and spending. Monetary policy is about the decisions made by central banks to control the amount of credit and money in circulation in an economy.

To spur growth in the economy, an example of a fiscal policy would be a stimulus program by the government to encourage spending, or a monetary policy where the central banks lower interest rates. The quantity theory of money is represented in the following formula:

Quantity of money * Volume of money = Price level * Real output

M*V = P*Y

We can also use the Fischer relationship, which is represented in the following formula:

Nominal interest rate = Real interest rate + Expected rate of inflation

RN = RR +πe

Central banks do not just control credit, they also store and release cash reserves to banks in their capacity as a lender of last resort. What this means is that if the economy is tough on banks and they cannot obtain financing from any other source, they can get loans from the central bank.

In their capacity, central banks apply different techniques to spur economic activity through monetary policy. One of these is to set the base lending rate at which banks can offer loans to their customers. They also trade treasury bonds to control the amount of money in the economy.

Central banks employ contractionary or expansionary monetary and fiscal policies. Expansionary policies reduce interest rates, hence increasing the amount of money in circulation. Contractionary policies do the opposite, and are used especially in periods of increasing inflation. Fiscal policies can be used to encourage economic growth and development through taxation, capital expenditure on things like infrastructure, or current spending in sectors like education, health, and the defense forces.

Governments can also spend through transfer payments, which are aimed at redistributing income in the economy through pensions, welfare programs, and any other similar cost units. However, such payments are not factored into GDP because there is no production taking place, just transfer of money from one sector to another.

International Trade

There are several benefits of international trade for participating countries, such as specialization, improving the quality of life and so forth.

International trade also breaks down monopolies, exposing consumers to better quality and variety.

International trade does have its challenges as well, such as losing market share for the local firms who cannot compete against stronger and wealthier competition from abroad.

Absolute advantage is a situation where one country can produce goods more cheaply than their competitors or trade partner. Comparative advantage is a situation where one country enjoys a lower opportunity cost in production. It is wise for countries to emphasize production in sectors where they enjoy comparative advantage, because of the efficiency in production, and the fact that this allows them to reduce cost of production, hence higher profit margins.

To protect the domestic and infant industries, countries can impose trade restrictions through tariffs, import quotas, and licensing regulations. This way, the imports are capped to protect the home market. This can also be done through capital control, limiting the amount of money coming in and out of the country. Countries that have weak or limited capital control regulations will often struggle to impose their monetary and fiscal policies, especially if their trading partners dwarf their economic power.

Trade between countries is captured in the Balance of Payments (BoP), a record of all transactions, in the following categories:

Current account – records the flow of goods and services

Capital account – records non-production and non-financial assets

Financial account – records all monetary assets

International trade takes place through the assistance of organizations like the IMF who sponsor member countries to stabilize their local monetary system, and WTO who fund development projects in member countries.

Foreign Currency Exchange

An exchange rate is a representation of the currency of one country over another. If the EUR/USD rate is 0.85, it means for every 1 USD, you can purchase 0.85 EUR. The base currency in this example is the USD, while the EUR is the price currency.

Immediate forex transactions are referred to as spot exchange rates, like the example above. A forward exchange rate refers to an exchange that will take place in the future, and are represented by basis points. One basis point is equivalent to 1/100th of a percentage. Therefore, conversion into decimal points means that you must divide by 10,000 as shown below:

Given USD/EUR Spot Rate of 1.8282

6-month forward points of 3

6-month forward rate = 1.8282 + (3/10,000) = 1.8285

Forward rates can also be represented as discounts or premiums to the spot rate, according to the relative interest rates between the participating countries. This is represented by the formula below:

$$F=S \{1+i(f)\}/\{1=i(d)\}$$

In this formula,

S – present spot rate

F – present forward rate

i(d) – domestic interest rate

i(f) – foreign interest rate

The formula for the premium rate is given as shown below:

Forward premium = S (1+x)

It is also possible to show exchange rates in terms of cross currency rates. In this case, we combine different exchange rates to arrive at a new rate.

The currency with the lowest interest rate should always be considered available at a forward premium.

Practice Questions and Answers

1. Consider the statements below about domestic income. Which of the two statements is most likely true?

Statement 1: A government's fiscal deficit carries a negative variance to domestic income

Statement 2: Net exports have a negative variance with the domestic price level and domestic income

A. Statement 1 and 2 are false

B. Statement 1 and 2 are true

C. Only one statement is false

The correct answer is B

Statement 1 and 2 are all true. An increase in a country's domestic income increases their imports, the result being a reduction in the net exports. If the domestic price level increases imports and exports decline in the process, the net exports also reduce. As the country's income increases, the income tax revenue also increases, which leads to a reduction in the budget deficit.

2. Which of the following statements gives a true description of a firm operating in a perfect competition market?

A. The firm is a price taker irrespective of the quantity being supplied to the market.

B. If the firm realizes they are recording low marginal revenues compared to the average fixed cost, they should stop production.

C. A breakeven point for the firm is a point where the marginal revenue is equal to the average variable cost.

The correct answer is A

In a perfect competition, there is free knowledge of the market. Firms and customers are well informed, so any firm operating in such a market will be a price taker, and this position is not affected by the quantity supplied in the market.

Statements B and C are not true. It is recommended that the firm shuts down production when they realize their marginal revenues are lower than the average variable cost, not the average fixed cost.

The firm will breakeven only when the marginal revenue is equal to the average total cost, not average variable cost.

3. The following information is derived from records of a given city for the year 2018 in millions. Using the information available, what is the household saving?

Consumer spending - $461,730

Government spending - $375,194

Personal income - $983,238

Personal disposable income - $534,109

Interest paid by consumers - $13,897

Consumer transfers to foreigners - $1,393

A. $35,385

B. $67,320

C. $57,089

The correct answer is C

Household saving is calculated in the following formula:

= Personal disposable income − (Consumption expenditure + Interest paid by customers + Personal transfer payments to foreigners)

= 534,109 − (461,730 + 13,897 + 1,393)

=57,089

4. The government is considering a strategy that will help to increase the amount of money in circulation within the economy. Which of the following actions is the government most unlikely to consider?

A. Announce a securities sale in an open market

B. Reduce the required reserve ratio

C. Reduce the prevailing discount rate

The correct answer is A

In an open market operation, the government can release more funds into the market by buying securities from the open market, not selling in an open market.

5. Companies that engage in international trade can be slapped with trade restrictions from time to time. When this happens, one of the effects is welfare loss for the affected importing company. Which of the restrictions below will affect the importing company the lowest?

A. Tariffs

B. Voluntary export restraint

C. Imposing quotas

The correct answer is A

When a tariff is imposed, the government still earns tariff revenue, which can offset the welfare loss. Voluntary export restraints involve quota rents that are received by the exporting country. When quotas are imposed, the rents are earned by both the importing and exporting countries.

6. The Heckscher-Ohlin model and Ricardian model are used when discussing factors of production. Which of the following statements reveals a common assumption about the factors of production shared by the two models?

A. Capital is not variable

B. The models consider homogenous inputs and homogenous products

C. Labor is variable

The correct answer is C

While the Heckscher-Ohlin model considers capital and labor as variable factors of production, the Ricardian model considers labor as a variable factor.

7. Which of the following descriptions is least likely to true of a giffen good?

A. A relationship between a change in quantity of goods demanded and a change in prices

B. A relationship between the effect of income changes and a change in prices

C. A relationship between the effect of substitution and a change in prices

The correct answer is C

For giffen goods, the following characteristics are true when the price reduces: a positive relation whereby the income effect causes a reduction in the quantity of goods demanded, a negative relation whereby the substitution effect causes an increase in the quantity of goods demanded, and a positive relation where the quantity demanded will fall because of the income effect.

8. Which of the following descriptions explain why an aggregate demand curve gets flat?

A. Investment expenditure is highly volatile in respect of interest rates.

B. Changes in income and interest rates have a high effect on the demand for money

C. Changes in income have a high effect on the level of savings in the economy

The correct answer is A

The following statements are true for a flattening aggregate demand curve. Investment expenditure is very sensitive with respect to changes in prevailing interest rates. The demand for money is insensitive to changes in interest rates and income. Savings are insensitive to income.

9. An electronics business sold 1,500 units and earned $600,000 in 2018. Upon estimation, they realized that if they sold 2,000 units, the total revenue earned would be $840,000. What would be the marginal cost per unit if they sold 2,000 units instead of 1,500 units?

A. $480

B. $450

C. $440

The correct answer is A

Marginal revenue

= Change in total revenue / Change in quantity

= (840,000 − 600,000) / (2,000 − 1,500)

= 240,000/500

= $480

10. An increase in aggregate demand is a sign that the economy is expanding. In such an economy, the investors would be highly unlikely to consider increasing their investment in which of the following areas?

A. Cyclical investments

B. Defense investments

C. Commodity-based investments

The correct answer is B

Given the fact that the economic data indicates the economy is expanding because of an increase in aggregate demand, there is a high likelihood that corporate profits in the market will increase. At the same time, the price for commodities will also increase, as will the prevailing interest rates. Over time, the market will be subject to inflationary pressure. It makes sense, therefore, that investors will choose to divest from defense projects because the possible profits from these investments will not increase as is expected of investments in cyclical projects.

Since the economy is expanding, investing in commodities, their markets, and cyclical investments would deliver higher yields, which makes them more attractive than defense investments.

11. Of the following market indicators, which one shows the average price of goods and services produced in the economy in a specific year?

A. Producer price index

B. Consumer price index

C. GDP deflator

The correct answer is C

The consumer price index is a measure of the changes in the price level of goods and services that consumers purchase. The producer price index is a measure of the average price changes that domestic producers receive for their products. The GDP deflator is a measure of the price of goods and services produced in the economy.

12. Which of the following represents the difference between the total variable cost producers incur and the total value buyers seek when purchasing goods?

A. Total surplus

B. Producer surplus

C. Consumer surplus

The correct answer is A

Total surplus is the sum of consumer and producer surplus. It is a representation of the difference in the consumer's total value and the producers' total variable cost. On the other hand, producer surplus refers to the difference between the total variable cost and the total revenue the producer earns. Consumer surplus represents the difference in value that the consumer expects from the products they purchase, and the cost of buying the goods.

13. The following statements attempt to describe a Stackelberg oligopoly. Which statement is the least likely untrue?

A. Participating firms are interdependent

B. Decision making by firms in the industry is sequential

C. No firm in the industry is capable of increasing their profits through a unilateral price change.

The correct answer is B

A Stackelberg oligopoly refers to a dominant firm. Decision making in this industry is sequential, unlike in a Cournot model which is characterized by simultaneous decision making.

In this scenario, the dominant firm is capable of unilaterally increasing their prices, thereby increasing their profits. Since the dominant firm enjoys great independence, all the firms in the market make their pricing decisions after the fact, based on the actions of the dominant firm.

14. Changes in the marginal returns to labor can explain a U-shaped curve in which of the following curves?

A. Short-run total product curve

B. Long-run AC curve

C. Short-run MC curve

The correct answer is C

Of the three curves, the total product curve does not form a U shape. At the beginning, it increases as rates increase, but further onwards, it will only increase with decreasing labor rates.

In the long run AC curve, the presence of a U-shaped curve can be an indication of economies of scale or diseconomies of scale.

Labor is a variable factor of production. Any changes to the marginal returns for such a factor of production can explain the U-shaped curve for the marginal cost and short run average cost curves.

15. Which of the following indicates the lowest point in a long-run average cost curve?

A. Econometric scale

B. Maximum efficient scale

C. Minimum efficient scale

The correct answer is A

The minimum efficient scale represents the lowest possible point in a long-run average cost curve. In a perfect competition, this is the optimal sustainable size for firms in the long run.

16. In a perfect competition, prices range between the average variable cost and the average total cost. From this assertion, what are the options that firms have when making decisions for the short-term and long-term?

A. Maintain operations in both the short term and long term

B. Maintain operations in the short term but leave the market in the long term

C. Close the business in the short term and exit the market in the long term

The correct answer is B

In a market where the prices range between the average variable costs and the average total costs, it makes sense that the firm maintains production in the short term. At this point, the firm is still able to meet all the running variable costs, and at the same time meet some of the fixed cost obligations.

In order for the firm to stay in the market in the long term, and still make profits while meeting all their costs, the firm has to breakeven. The only way this can happen is if the price is equal to the average total costs.

17. The absorption approach is used to explain the effect that changes in the prevailing exchange rates have on trade balance. This approach most likely explains one of the following:

A. A microeconomic perspective that explains the relationship between trade balance and exchange rates in the economy.

B. The impact of changes in exchange rates on saving decisions or the aggregate expenditure.

C. The impact of changes in the relative prices of foreign and domestic goods.

The correct answer is B

There are two methods that can be used to examine the effect of a change in exchange rates on the trade balance, the absorption approach or the elasticities approach.

In the absorption approach, the emphasis is on the effect of changes in the exchange rates on savings decisions or aggregate expenditure.

In the elasticities approach, the emphasis is on the effect of changes in the relative price of foreign and domestic goods. This approach represents a microeconomic perspective of the relationship between trade balance and exchange rates.

18. The following characteristics represent a firm that is operating in a monopolistic competition.

Which is the most likely correct characteristic?

A. Many sellers, low barriers to entry, no profits in the long run

B. Very few sellers, low barriers to entry, no profits in the long run

C. Very few sellers, high barriers to entry, positive profits in the long run

The correct answer is A

In monopolistic competition, the fact that there is no entry barrier attracts many sellers to the market, and as more sellers enter the market, the profits decline to a point where there is no long-term profit.

Chapter 4: Financial Reporting and Analysis

This chapter contains actionable knowledge on alternative investments, including real estate, private equity, commodities, infrastructure, and hedge funds. You will distinguish their unique features and learn how to include them in your portfolio.

Analyzing financial statements is an important procedure through which you learn how to assess the financial position of your company, and the risks the business faces during the trading period. It is important to remember that there are different reporting standards applicable to different companies in different parts of the world, bearing in mind the fact that the reporting approaches and principles are not universally acceptable.

To analyze financial statements, you must be in a position to study and interpret the financial results of the company in light of the realities of the economy the company is operating in, make comparisons with relevant companies in the market, and identify issues that might arise in the statements at your disposal, especially proof of manipulation.

Financial Statement Analysis

Financial statement analysis refers to a process where you examine the performance of the company in light of the prevalent economic standards and make recommendations or decisions based on the information. This analysis helps you determine the capital position of the company, or whether you can invest in their securities and debt. As a debt investor, your concern is whether the company is profitable enough to pay back the debt owed plus the accrued interest. Equity securities investors, on the other hand, are interested in determining whether the company is profitable enough to earn them dividends, and whether they feel the company is stable enough so they can increase their shareholding.

Important financial reports for this analysis include audited financial statements, disclosures as per the regulatory principles in the jurisdiction of the company, and any commentaries that might not be audited, which the company sees fit to include and help the users gain a better understanding of the organization's operations.

Company financial reporting is meant to provide information about the financial position of the company, the performance of the company, and changes in the company's financial position in light of different stimuli in the business operating environment.

With this information, analysts can determine the future of the company based on the present and past performance information, and an analysis of the current business environment.

Analysts access financial reports to make the following decisions:

Determine future projections for cash flow and net revenue.

Making investment decisions based on security valuation.

Determine the appropriate debt rating for the company.

Allow credit facilities to customers.

Determine the company's compliance standards in light of debt and other contractual implications.

Determine the equity investment value.

Evaluate the position of the company in light of a possible merger.

Determine the creditworthiness of the company.

In as much as the profitability status of the company is of key interest to investors, it is equally important to ensure the company can continue providing positive cashflow to sustain the suppliers, employees, and keep operating as a going concern. Besides, generating positive cash flows from operations is a sign that the company is flexible and can enter into investments that have attractive returns in the future.

Financial statements are prepared at different, regular intervals providing useful information to internal and external users. For a financial statement to be complete, it must include the following:

Balance sheet – statement of the financial position

Income statement – statement of comprehensive income

Cash flow statement

Statement of changes in equity

Relevant footnotes and notes on the financial statements

Additional information in the form of commentaries from the management

Report from an external editor

Governance report explaining the makeup of the board of directors

Balance sheet

This is the statement of the company's financial position. It discloses all the company's assets and debt obligations at a given point in time. The balance sheet highlights the company's assets and liabilities against the owner's equity. The owner's equity is a statement of the company's position after honoring their liabilities. This can be expressed as follows:

Assets = Liabilities + Owners' Equity

The equation above is also referred to as the accounting or balance sheet equation. In some cases, and depending on the structure of the company, owners' equity can also be referred to as capital, shareholders' equity or partners' capital.

From the balance sheet, an analyst can compare two or more financial reporting periods and deduce the following information:

Whether the company's liquidity position has improved or not, which affects the company's ability to meet their obligations.

Determine the company's financial standing in light of the prevailing economic conditions in the industry.

Determine whether the company is solvent – if it has sufficient resources to meet the obligations.

Income Statement

The income statement gives information on the financial performance of the company over a given trading period. It indicates the revenue generated by the company against the expenses incurred in earning that revenue.

The expense statements indicate all the cash outflows, liabilities, and asset depletion which reduce the company's equity. This includes administrative expenses, cost of sales, income tax expenses, and any other expenditure information that might be made available.

Net earnings refer to the bottom line of the company once the expenses and income have been accounted for. From the income generated during the accounting period, account for the expenses incurred and remain with the net income. The net earnings can be a profit or a loss.

Income statements are prepared in consolidation, and as a result, might include statements from subsidiaries of the reporting company. The basic accounting equation for the income statement is presented as follows:

Revenue + Other Income − Expenses = Income − Expenses = Net Income

Parent companies must, therefore, present their income statements as consolidated statements that include the statements of the subsidiary companies.

From the income statement, an analyst can deduce information including the following:

Whether the company can compete against other companies in the industry.

In the case of a company with multiple business units, how each of the units' revenue position changes and affects the parent company.

Find a credible explanation for the change in the company's revenue position.

The statement of comprehensive income can include other information beyond what is available in the income statement. This refers to any activity that affects the owners' equity, but do not arise as a result of transactions with shareholders.

Statement of changes in equity

This statement provides information on the changes in the owners' investment in the company over the trading period. More importantly, the statement focuses on the retained earnings and paid-in capital.

Retained earnings refer to the profits the company retains instead of paying out in dividends. In the equity segment, the report includes minority reserves and interests in the company which represent comprehensive income or other accumulated income.

The statement of changes in equity highlights for every equity item, the opening balance, any changes (positive or negative) during the trading period, and the closing balance.

In the case of paid-in capital, for example, a new equity issue increases the capital. If the company repurchases stocks that were previously issued, this indicates a decrease in paid-in capital.

In the case of retained earnings, paying out dividends decreases the earnings, while net income from the income statement and any other comprehensive income increases the retained earnings.

Cash flow statement

While you can determine the financial position of the company from the balance sheet and income statement, the cash flow statement is equally important in analyzing the long-term prospects of the company.

From the cash flow statement, debtors, creditors and other investors can determine the solvency and liquidity position of the company, and determine how flexible it is financially.

Financial flexibility simply indicates whether the company can adapt to financial challenges or take advantage of opportunities when they arise. This statement groups the company's cash flows in the following categories:

Operating cash flows – They involve cash flows that determine the net income, or daily operations of the company.

Investing cash flows – These are cash flows from any activities involving disposing of company assets (especially long-term assets), or new acquisitions. They include things like property and equipment cash flows.

Financing cash flows – These are cash flows from any activities in the company that involve gains or repayments of capital used to run the business.

Notes to financial statements

Notes to financial statements can be available either as notes or footnotes. They are important, as they help to shed more light on the prepared financial statements. They help users understand the statements.

Notes disclose useful information like important factors that were considered in preparing the statements. They also provide information like the accounting methods, estimates, and policies used in preparing the financial statements.

Companies must be flexible when preparing these statements, in order to meet their unique needs, such as events, and transactions. Flexibility is important when preparing financial statements, as it allows the company to choose the applicable methods, policies, and estimates that are relevant to their operations, and unique to the economy the company is operating in.

Because of flexibility in preparing financial statements, it might not be easy to make comparisons between two or more companies without the notes to the financial statements. It is only credible to compare companies when their statements are prepared in unison over the trading periods in question.

If this happens, a financial analyst can easily compare the companies and determine differences beyond their accounting choices. This is why notes to financial statements are useful. An analyst can use this information to guide their decisions when comparing financial statements for the companies. For example, Company A and Company B might purchase the same equipment, but use different assumptions or methods to record expenses accrued in using the equipment over its useful life. These differences impede the ability of an analyst to compare the performance of the two companies, unless it is expressed in the notes.

When preparing the notes to financial statements, the estimates, methods, and policies that determine the accounting choices must be expressed. Other than that, the following information can also be provided:

Performance of different operating segments.

Disposals and acquisitions.

Subsequent events (events that happen after the date of the balance sheet).

Transactions involving parties to the company.

Contingencies.

Commitments.

Legal proceedings.

Financial instruments.

Risks arising out of financial instruments.

The analyst must be careful when analyzing and judging the financial statements, in light of the notes and disclosures present.

Management commentary

This statement is present in financial reports of publicly held companies. In this section, the management addresses any issues that might be of concern to the company in the past, present, or future. Other than the financial statements themselves, this is one of the important parts of the reports, though they are usually unaudited. Before using this information, the financial analyst must ascertain whether it is audited or not.

Auditor's report

An independent auditing firm must go through the financial statements before they are presented, to ensure they are in accordance with specific auditing standards. After verifying the content of the reports, the auditor presents an audit report, which is their opinion piece on the financial statements.

The role of the auditor in this case under the International Standards for Auditing (ISA) is to provide assurance on the financial statements, proving they are free from fraudulent or erroneous misstatement.

Framework for Financial Statement Analysis

There are different kinds of financial analysts in investment management. It is important to understand their roles, especially in determining the attractiveness of a venture or investment. The following is a breakdown of how this happens:

Understand the purpose and context of the analysis

Collect the relevant data input

Data processing

Interpretation of the processed data

Formulating conclusions and recommendations from the data

Following up.

Financial reporting

As mentioned earlier, business activities are classified into three categories: operating activities, investing activities and financing activities. When you understand the nature of business activities, it is easier for you to determine how the company is run, and whether or not it is profitable, or will be profitable in the long run.

From an investment perspective, a sound company is one that generates most of the profits from operating activities. It is important to understand how different transactions from business activities are reported in the financial records.

Business activities are recorded as either revenue, liabilities, assets, owners' equity or expenses. Economic resources of the company are assets. Liabilities are the claims creditors have on the economic resources of the company. Owners' equity refers to the residual claim on the resources once the creditors' claims are settled. Revenues refer to the cash inflows from the assets, while expenses are the cash outflows from the use of company assets, or an increase in the company liabilities.

An account is the individual record of an increase or decrease in an asset, liability, expense, revenue, or an element of owners' equity. Companies keep different accounts for different purposes. The following is a breakdown of the components of different company accounts:

Assets

Cash equivalents and cash

Prepaid expenses

Trade and accounts receivables

Inventory

Tax assets (deferred or current)

Intangible assets like goodwill, copyright and patents

Investment property

Equipment, plant and property

Liabilities

Debts payable

Trade and accounts payable

Accrued liabilities

Provisions
Financial liabilities
Bonds payable
Unearned income
Reserves
Deferred or current tax liabilities
Owners' equity
Minority interest
Capital
Retained earnings
Other comprehensive income
Paid-up capital
Revenue
Sales
Gains
Investment income
Expenses
Losses
Tax expenses
Cost of inventory
Administrative, general and selling expenses
Amortization
Depreciation
Interest expense
In financial statements, assets are classified as current or non-current assets. Non-current assets should benefit the company over a period of more than one year. They can include things like goodwill, equipment, property and investments held in different companies.

Current assets, on the other hand, are held with a view of immediate or near-immediate consumption or conversion into cash in a period less than one year. They include inventory, commercial, and accounts receivables.

Receivables are amounts that other parties owe the company. They might be owed by customers or other parties. Cash equivalents refer to short-term investments that mature in less than 90 days.

Accounting Equations

The balance sheet equation is presented as

Assets = Liabilities + Owners' Equity

This is proof that only owners' equity and liabilities hold claims on company assets.

Owners' equity can also be represented in terms of net assets, net worth, net book value or partners' capital depending on the type of company.

However, the balance sheet equation still remains the same.

In light of the above, Owners' equity = Contributed Capital + Retained earnings

In the income statement, the business performance over a given trading period is represented by the income statement equation below:

Net Income or Loss = Revenue – Expenses

Revenue can also be represented by other terms like turnover, or sales. Net income can be represented as net earnings or net profit.

The balance sheet gives the financial position of the company at a specific trading point, while the income statement informs us of the company's activity over the said time. Together, these statements provide information on retained earnings.

The opening retained earnings refers to the balance in the retained earnings account when the accounting period opens, and ending retained earnings is the closing balance at the end of the trading period. To calculate the retained earnings for a given trading period, you include the beginning balance, the net income and any distributions or dividends paid out to the company shareholders. This gives us the equation below:

Closing retained earnings = Opening retained earnings + Net income – Dividends

Or

Closing retained earnings = Opening retained earnings + Revenue – Expenses – Dividends

As you can tell from the name, retained earnings are earnings that are held by the company. They are not distributed as dividends. This can further be represented by combining the information in the balance sheet and the income statement to result in the following equation:

Assets = Liabilities + Capital contribution + Closing retained earnings

Or

Assets = Liabilities + Capital contribution + Opening retained earnings + Revenue – Expenses – Dividends

The equations above show us the statement of retained earnings, the connection between the income statement and balance sheet. In a simple example below, the company had the following records in their financial statements:

Opening retained earnings $2500

Net income $2000

No dividends were paid

Closing retained earnings = $2500 + $2000 - $0 = $4500

This brings us to another important element of accounting: double-entry accounting. Under this principle, each accounting transaction will always affect at least two accounts to maintain a balance. For example, when you purchase an equipment in cash, two asset accounts are involved (the equipment account and the cash account). The equipment account increases with the cash value paid to acquire the equipment, while the cash account decreases by the said cash value.

If you offset a liability in cash, the liability account and the cash account are affected. The liability account decreases and the cash account also decreases by the said amount. Since two accounts are affected, the accounting equation should balance, which is the basic accounting principle. Let's look at the example below.

A company's records reveal the following information:

Liabilities at the end of the year = $10,000

Capital contribution at the end of the year = $10,000

Retained earnings at the beginning of the year = $5,000

Revenue earned during the year = $40,000

Expenditure during the year = $ 38,000

No dividends were distributed to the owners.

Determine the company's total assets at the end of the year.

Solution

The closing retained earnings

= Opening retained earnings + Revenue – Expenses

= $5,000 + $40,000 - $38,000 = $7,000

Total assets at the end of the year = Liabilities + Capital contribution + Closing retained earnings

= $10,000 + $10,000 + $7,000 = $27,000

Accounting Process

In accounting processes, business transactions are recorded in a manner that allows clear and concise reporting for financial statements. All the records are eventually combined to create the financial statements presented at the end of the trading period. Accounting systems incorporate all the financial activities associated with the business and present the final report in a usable financial record. When analyzing accounts, the following are the important events that you must follow as an analyst:

Determine the accounts affected by a specified amount.

Establish the type of account

Enter the correct information in the reporting spreadsheet

Verify to ensure your accounting equation is balanced.

Accruals and adjustments for valuation

Many business transactions are cash-based, and can be reported in a very short time. It is easy to account for transactions that take place within the same financial period. However, in some cases transactions spread to other trading periods, in which case you have to make adjustments for their valuation. This is common where a disbursement or cash is received in one period but the expenditure or revenue is earned in another. For such situations, accruals and valuation adjustments are necessary.

Accruals

This is an accounting principle that demands that expenses must be recorded when the business incurs them, while revenue is only recorded when you earn it. This way, revenues and expenditures are reported in the right trading period.

Deferred or unearned revenues arise in a situation where the company is paid for services or products before they earn that revenue. A good example is a subscription model. When the company is paid in full for a 12-month subscription, the service is fully paid for, but it is yet to be rendered. The company only earns the revenue at the end of each month, until the full amount is earned at the end of the 12 months.

Accrued or unbilled revenues arise when the company has earned the revenue before they receive payment, but the revenue is not yet recognized at the close of their financial year. Prepaid expenses arise when the company pays in cash for a product or service, before they recognize the expense. An example is paying for rent one month ahead of schedule. These are assets but they will eventually be expensed at a later data. Accrued expenses arise when the company is billed for expenses that by the end of the financial period, are yet to be paid. They are liabilities, because they must be paid for at a later date.

Valuation adjustments

While accrual entries account for expenses and revenue in the correct accounting periods, valuation adjustments are only made to the assets and liabilities of the company where accounting standards demand so, and in order to provide the real market value of the company at the reporting time, instead of the historical or future value.

In case you need to make valuation adjustments for company assets, you increase the asset on one side of the equation and on the income statement you indicate a gain. In the event of asset decrease, you decrease one side of the equation and record a loss on the income statement.

Accounting Systems

Foundation accounting systems are basic in nature. However, over time they become more complex in response to unique company needs. The flow of accounting records and statements takes place in four steps as outlined below:

Step 1: Journal entries

All business transactions are recorded in journal entries in chronological order according to the date of the transaction. The journals reflect the accounts, amounts, and dates affected. In some cases, it is wise to provide a brief explanation of the transactions for future use.

Any information that is yet to be reflected in the accounting system can be presented in the form of adjusting journal entries.

Step 2: General ledger accounts

General ledger accounts are files that show different transactions in the business according to their accounts. The general ledger is basically the foundation of any accounting system.

The difference between journals and ledgers is that journals sort transactions according to the date, while the general ledger sorts transactions according to the account.

Step 3: Adjusted trial balance

The trial balance shows all the account balances at a specific time. It is the first statement prepared at the end of the accounting period, and helps in preparing financial statements. While ledgers show a lot of information about transactions, trial balances only show the final account balances.

Step 4: Financial statements

This is the final product in the accounting system, according to the totals in different accounts, and balances from the adjusted trial balance.

In every accounting transaction, there is always a debit and credit transaction taking place at any given time, because as one account increases, another must decrease in the affected value.

Security Analysis Through Financial Statements

Financial analysts need financial statements to help in their valuation of the company. In your position as an analyst, you might be privy to some information that was not presented in the financial statements. In this case, you have to make adjustments to reflect them. Common information you will make adjustments for include future earnings, and some assets or liabilities.

One of the biggest challenges for an analyst is identifying deliberate manipulation of accounts. Beyond that, however, you will also have to study the prevailing economic trends to determine the accurate position of the company, over and above any information available in the financial statements.

The most important step in establishing the authenticity of financial statements is to determine the nature of the accruals and valuation entries.

The annual report contains most of this information. You can use this to determine the important valuations or accruals in the statements you have. Many companies attempt to achieve a desired outcome in their financial statements by misquoting transactions. A common example is when the company spends cash on something, but instead of recording it as an expense, they reduce the cash and increase their asset accounts to show they recorded higher income. In such an example, the right side of the balance sheet is not affected by the transaction, because it balances out on the opposite side.

In essence what such companies do is they intentionally reduce their operating expenditure, and recharge some expenditure accounts as capital assets. What this does is that you end up with a lower expense account, and a false identity of a high income at the end of the trading period, when the real scenario is very different.

Today, thanks to technological advancements, many of the accounting software in use cannot allow direct manipulation where you make entries on one side of the accounting system and do not reflect the same on the opposite side. However, this does not mean that crafty accountants or companies do not do it.

It is possible to manipulate some accounts to deliver a specific outcome that eventually balances the books, but the true account of the financial statements shows a different picture. Let's say the accountant needs to account for a false revenue. All they have to do is create a false receivable account so the equation balances. Assuming some money was paid out for something that the company does not wish to disclose in their books, the amount can be indicated in a prepaid asset account.

As an analyst, for you to establish these unscrupulous deals, you must first realize that for every entry in the financial statements, there must always be a corresponding entry on the opposite side. In order to fix accounts, most careless accountants fail to account for the corresponding entry because when they do, their accounts will not balance.

Financial Reporting Standards

The goal behind financial reporting is to ensure analysts have access to critical information about the company, useful information that is relevant to lenders, investors, and creditors.

Accounting standards boards are present in every market in the world. They institute policies that outline how companies report financial statements. The key accounting standards boards are as follows:

International Accounting Standards Board (IASB)

Financial Accounting Standards Board (FASB)

Regulatory authorities

These are government agencies and entities whose legal mandate allows them to enforce regulations and control the operations of companies under their jurisdiction, so that participation in capital markets takes place transparently. They include the following:

International Organization of Securities Commissions (IOSCO)

The Securities and Exchange Commission (SEC)

Capital Markets Regulation in the EU

In line with the reporting standards and requirements of the regulatory authorities, the following are the key features of financial statements:

No offsetting – incomes, expenditures, assets and liabilities must never be offset unless it is necessary or allowed by the IFRS.

Accrual reporting – other than cash flow information, all financial statements must be prepared in the accrual accounting format.

Presentation – all transactions must be recorded to show the truthful position of assets, liabilities, income and expenditure.

Going concern – unless the company is to be liquidated, all financial statements must be prepared as a going concern.

Aggregation and materiality – any misstatement or omission from the financial statements must be declared, especially if they affect the decisions of intended users of the financial statements.

Reporting frequency – companies must prepare financial statements at least once a year.

Consistency – the classification and presentation of contents in the financial statement must be the same across different accounting periods.

Company Disclosures

Companies are required to disclose vital information about their financial statements and business operations. Where necessary, this is in the notes to the financial statements. There are different kinds of disclosures expected of companies, as follows:

Disclosures concerning critical accounting policies

When addressing these disclosures, the following factors should be taken into consideration:

Which policies are affected?

Has the company made any changes to the policies over the years?

Will changes to the policies affect key balances on the financial statements?

Which are the policies that require specific estimates?

Disclosures concerning changes in accounting policies

Companies are required to disclose any information regarding changes to their accounting policies. This happens when the company institutes a new accounting standard, or if they elect to change specific policies in their books. These changes include:

Standards that are no longer applicable to the company.

Standards whose adoption has been discussed.

Standards whose impact is still under review by management.

Standards that might not have an impact.

Practice Questions and Answers

1. A company purchased machinery on 1st January 2015 for $400,000. Upon delivery, the machine was leased out through a direct finance lease, whose

terms were five annual payments of $99,074 beginning 1st January 2015. The purchase price of the machinery is equal to the carrying price, and the discount rate is 14%. Which of the following is the closest lease receivable from the machinery as at 1st January 2016?

A. $56,944

B. $243,982

C. $300,926

The correct answer is B

Annual lease receivable deduction = Annual lease payment – Accrued interest

1st January 2015

Lease receivable deduction

= 99,074 – 0

= $99,074

Lease receivable value

= 400,000 – 99,074

= $300,926

1st January 2016

Lease receivable deduction

= 99,074 – (300,926 x 14%)

= $56,944

Lease receivable value

= 300,926 – 56,944

= $243,982

2. The following statements represent accounting methods, estimates and assumptions, and information about management and director compensation. Which statement is true?

A. Accounting methods, estimates and assumptions are found in the footnotes section. Management and director compensation are presented in the proxy statement.

B. Accounting methods, estimates and assumptions are found in the footnotes section. Management and director compensation are presented in the management discussion and analysis statement.

C. Accounting methods, estimates and assumptions are found in the management discussion and analysis statement. Management and director compensation are presented in the auditor's report.

The correct answer is A

Any information about accounting methods used, estimates and assumptions that apply when preparing financial statements are usually found in the footnotes to the financial statements.

Any information about compensation for management and directors is usually presented in the proxy statement.

3. Which of the following statements cannot be used to classify cash receipts in a company under IFRS guidelines?

A. Financing activity

B. Investment activity

C. Operating activity

The correct answer is A

Under the IFRS, companies can classify cash receipts as investment or operating activities.

4. Your company has released payment in cash for an expense item, but that expenditure is not recognized in the financial statements yet. What will be the most accurate statement about this payment?

A. Recognize the payment as a liability, an accrued revenue

B. Recognize the payment as an asset, a prepaid expense.

C. Recognize the payment as an asset, an accrued expense

The correct answer is B

By paying for the expense in cash before it is recognized in the accounting books, the company creates a prepaid expense, which is an asset.

5. A local construction company is contracted to build an administrative block. The construction should cost around $40 million over three years. However, the situation on the ground is different, and there are lots of uncertainties about the project, making it difficult to accurately determine the project output. By the end of the first year, the company has recorded expenditure of $34 million. How would the company recognize the payments under GAAP?

A. Increase the inventory account by $34 million

B. Indicate the cost of construction as $34 million

C. Indicate $0 in all accounts until the construction is completed after three years.

The correct answer is A

Following the GAAP guidelines, the company is expected to realize $0 in revenue at the end of the first year. The company will also record $0 income and $0 cost of construction in their accounting books. However, the $34 million spent on construction will be included in the books as a decrease in the cash account, and a subsequent increase in the inventory accounts, if the company made payments in cash.

6. In the year 2014, the local government contracted a company to build a bridge, a project that was expected to last for 5 years. The information about the project was as follows:

Cost incurred in 2014 - $4,000,000

Total cost of the project - $24,000,000

Total revenue from the project - $30,000,000

The project's outcome cannot be reliably determined, but the revenue recorded in 2014 was recognized under IFRS and GAAP. Which of the following statements is true about the revenue recognition?

A. IFRS $4,000,000. GAAP $0

B. IFRS $0 GAAP $0

C. IFRS $4,000,000 GAAP $4,000,000

The correct answer is A

The first thing you must realize about this question is that it took place in 2014, after the release of the converged standards.

Based on that assertion, if it is impossible to provide a reliable assessment of the outcome for a long-term project, the following conditions apply:

IFRS – Revenue is only recognized in as far as the costs incurred during the period in question are concerned.

GAAP – The principle of project completion applies. Therefore, you do not recognize revenue until the project is completed.

7. Instead of expensing expenditure, the directors at Shell Corporation agreed to capitalize their expenditure. As a result of this decision, which of the following will reduce?

A. Cash outflow from operations
B. Debt to equity
C. Total assets

The correct answer is A

If the company capitalizes their expenditure, the following will happen in that accounting period. Before the company feels the effect of depreciation charges, their total assets will initially reduce. Their cash outflows from operation will also decline. Initially, the debt to equity ratio is not affected by this decision. However, by the end of the accounting period, the NBV of the company assets will be reduced because of the depreciation charges.

8. The following information is available about a company that prepares their accounts following the GAAP:

Opening shareholders' equity	$3,000,000
Net income	$500,000
Declared dividends	$150,000
Paid dividends	$180,000

Closing shareholders' equity $4,000,000
What is the company's comprehensive income for that year?
A. $650,000
B. $1,150,000
C. $150,000
The correct answer is B
Other comprehensive income
= Closing shareholders' equity + Declared dividends – Net Income – Opening shareholders' equity
= 4,000,000 + 150,000 – 500,000 – 3,000,000
= 650,000
Comprehensive income
= Net income + Other comprehensive income
= 500,000 + 650,000
= $1,150,000
9. The following statements describe possibilities when auditing financial statements. Which of the statements is most probably true?
A. In the event of an unqualified opinion, the role of an auditor is to offer absolute assurance regarding the precision and accuracy of financial statements.
B. An auditor can issue a qualified opinion about unreported pending contingent liabilities if he harbors concerns about them.
C. A disclaimer of opinion refers to a situation where the auditor presents their opinion irrespective of limitations to their scope.
The correct answer is B

An independent auditor is unable to issue absolute assurance as to the precision and accuracy of financial statements, even if their opinion is not qualified. Auditors, however, are allowed to provide a qualified opinion if they are concerned about the following:

The valuation of some items in the balance sheet
Pending contingent liabilities that have not been reported
The ability of the company to continue operations as a going concern

A disclaimer of opinion is apparent in a situation where an auditor cannot issue an opinion because of the scope of limitation, or any other such reason.

10. The following information is available about a company in the financial year ending 31st December, 2018. What is the free cash flow for the year?

Investment in working capital $1,150,000	
Paid dividends	$250,000
Net capital expenditure	$1,750,000
Prevailing tax rate	40%
Net income	$12,500,000
Amortization	$500,000
Depreciation	$1,250,000
Interest expenditure	$3,000,000

A. $9,500,000
B. $13,150,000
C. $16,250,000
The correct answer is B
Free cash flow

= 12,500,000 + 1,750,000 + (3,000,000 × [1 – 0.4])
– 1,750,000 – 1,150,000
= $13,150,000

11. You are asked to prepare the financial statements for your company under the GAAP standards. Based on the records available, you find it prudent to classify securities as available for sale securities. Following the same precedence, what is the appropriate treatment for unrealized losses and gains?

A. Recognize unrealized losses and gains as equity, but do not report them in the income statement.

B. Do not recognize unrealized losses and gains as equity. Do not report them in the income statement.

C. Report unrealized losses and gains in the income statement.

The correct answer is A

Under GAAP, securities that are classified as available for sale are securities that are identified at their fair market value. For this reason, unrealized losses and gains are recognized as equity, but not reported in the income statement.

12. An accountant at a manufacturing plant is tasked with handling reversals for inventory write-downs. Which of the following statements most likely represents their best course of action under GAAP and IFRS?

A. Not allowed under GAAP. Not allowed under IFRS

B. Not allowed under GAAP. Allowed under IFRS, with the limit set at the previous write-down.

C. Allowed under GAAP, with the limit set at the previous write-down. Allowed under IFRS, and the previous recognized amount can be less than the new value.

The correct answer is B

The following rules apply for any company that is not engaged in agricultural or mining activities:

GAAP does not allow reversal of inventory write-downs

IFRS allows the reversal, but only to the limit of the previous write-down that was recorded.

13. Jim is delivering 10 computers to his client at $4,500 each. The total amount Jim will charge for the computers is $43,000, and he expects to be paid in 45 days. At the time the computers are delivered, Jim was not paid any amount in cash. What is the appropriate accounting treatment that will take place at the time of delivery?

A. Reduce inventory by $43,000 and increase revenue and accounts receivable by $45,000

B. Increase revenue account by $4,500, reduce the cost of goods sold account by $43,000 but the cash account will remain unchanged.

C. Increase the revenue and accounts receivable account by $45,000, and reduce the cost of goods sold and inventory account by $43,000

The correct answer is A

At the time Jim is delivering the computers to his client, the following activities happen in their accounts:

Cost of goods sold account increased by $43,000
Inventory account reduced by $43,000
Revenue and accounts receivable account increased by $45,000

14. When preparing the financial statements for your company, which of the following statements gives a true picture of the position of depreciation for property, plant and equipment under GAAP and IFRS?

A. You must review the useful life and residual value in both GAAP and IFRS

B. You must review the useful life and residual value in GAAP but not IFRS

C. You must assess every component of an asset and factor in depreciation separately under IFRS, but not GAAP

The correct answer is C

The IFRS standards demand an annual review of the useful life and residual value for property, plant and equipment, which is not the case in GAAP.
Each component of an asset has to be depreciated individually under IFRS, which is not the case for GAAP.

15. The following statements define the position of a company:

S1 – During the first year of operation, the cost of goods available for sale under LIFO and FIFO will be the same in a situation where the prices of the goods have been falling all through the year.

S2 – If prices have been falling all through the year, the company can save more money if they use LIFO

Which of the two statements is least unlikely?

A. S1 is untrue

B. S2 is untrue

C. S1 and S2 are untrue

The correct answer is B

The cost of goods available for sale refers to the sum of inventory at the beginning of the trading period and any purchases made during that period. In a trading period where prices have been falling, companies that use LIFO will have a lower cost of goods sold, which translates to more net income, higher spending on taxes and lower cash reserves. During the first year of operation, the assumption of inventory cost flow does not affect the total amount recorded as cost of goods available for sale.

16. At the end of the financial year 2018, a financial analyst was presented with the following information about a company.

Net income	$40 million
Prevailing tax rate	40%
Capital expenditure	$12 million
Interest paid after tax	$4.5 million
Cash flow from operations	$18 million
Non-cash charges	$9 million

Determine the free cash flow for the company.

A. $6 million

B. $10.5 million
C. $22 million
The correct answer is B
Free cash flow
= Cash flow from operations + Interest paid after tax − Capital expenditure
= 18 million + 4.5 million − 12 million
= 10.5 million

17. Paul is hired by Apollo Investments as a financial advisor. The company's management has tasked him with determining the best way for the company to report higher earnings over the coming years. Which of the following is the most likely resolution Paul will report to management?

A. Reduce the assets' useful life and increase the estimated salvage value

B. Reduce the estimated salvage value of the assets and extend the assets' useful life

C. Increase the estimated salvage value of assets by extending the assets' useful life

The correct answer is C

By recognizing a low depreciation expense, the company can increase their earnings. To do this, they must first increase the useful life estimate for the assets, and increase the estimated salvage value.

18. How are you least likely to handle impairment loss in your financial statements?

A. Recognize impairment loss as a non-cash item, so it will not reflect in the cash flow statement

B. Impairment loss reduces the carrying amount on assets and the net income

C. Impairment loss reduces the cash flow during the year you record a loss

The correct answer is C

Impairment does not recur, and for this reason, you do not consider it for future analytical projections. Options A and B are correct.

19. While preparing financial statements for 2016, an asset's value was revalued downwards. In the following year 2017, the value of the asset was revalued upwards. What is the most probable effect that these actions will have on the reported return on equity and leverage?

A. Return on equity increases as the reported leverage improves

B. Return on equity increases as the reported leverage worsens

C. Return on equity decreases as the reported leverage improves

The correct answer is A

According to the IFRS method of revaluation, if a recent downward revaluation is reversed by an upward revaluation, the recognized gains are realized in the income statement as an increase in the net income realized. This also means shareholding equity will increase.

In case the upward revaluation was not aimed at reversing recent downward revaluation, the realized gains will be recognized as revaluation surplus, and will only increase shareholding equity.

In 2017, the reported leverage ratios decrease because the assets and shareholding equity increase.

Since the shareholding equity and net income increases, the return on equity will also increase. This is because of a dominant numerator effect, hence an increase in the ratio.

20. Instead of using the double declining balance depreciation method, JAG Inc. accountants prefer the straight-line method. During the early years of their assets, the following ratios were implemented. Which of them will most likely have a low result?

A. Asset turnover

B. Operating return on assets

C. Operating profit margin

The correct answer is A

Companies that use the straight-line method of depreciation will have the following in their reports:

Low depreciation expense, hence a higher operating return on assets

Low depreciation expense, hence a higher operating profit margin

High net assets, hence low turnover on assets

21. During the year 2018, the average market price for Yale Corp stock was $80, and the price at the end of the year was $90. A careful analysis of their accounting books revealed the following information:

20,000 ordinary shares had warrants, and their exercise price was $60

40,000 ordinary shares had options, and their exercise price was $40

From this information, which of the following is the true number of inferred shares that will help in determining diluted earnings per share?

A. 5,000

B. 25,000

C. 20,000

The correct answer is B

The exercise price for the options and warrants are below the average market price for Yale Corp stock through the year. Therefore, the options and warrants are dilutive.

Warrants:

= 60 x 20,000 = 1,200,000

Repurchased shares at the average market price

= 1,200,000 / 80 = 15,000

Outstanding shares net increase

= 20,000 – 15,000 = 5,000

Options:

= 40 x 40,000 = 1,600,000

Repurchased shares at average market price

= 1,600,000 / 80 = 20,000

Outstanding shares net increase

= 40,000 – 20,000 = 20,000

Number of inferred shares

= 5,000 + 20,000 = 25,000

22. The following describes the qualities of an effective financial reporting framework. Which of the characteristics below is the most unlikely?

A. Transparency

B. Consistency

C. Comparability

The correct answer is C

An effective financial reporting framework is characterized by consistency, comprehensiveness, and transparency. Comparability, on the other hand, refers to one of four supplementary qualitative features of financial statements.

23. When preparing income statements, which of the following items will be unlikely to be expressed as a fraction of sales?

A. Depreciation

B. Income taxes

C. Interest expense

The correct answer is B

While depreciation and interest expense can be expressed as a fraction of sales, income taxes are often expressed as a fraction of income before tax

24. When preparing financial statements under IFRS, which of the following statements represent an identifiable intangible asset?

A. The intangible asset must be within the control of the company, hence identifiable. The company must also derive future economic benefits from an intangible asset.

B. You must be able to reliably determine the cost of the asset.

C. The expectation of the asset is that the company will realize economic benefits in the future

The correct answer is A

The IFRS guidelines recognize an identifiable intangible asset if it meets the following characteristics:

It can be identified.

The company controls it.

The company expects economic benefits from the asset in the future.

The asset must also meet the following recognition criteria:

The company can reliably determine the cost of the intangible asset

The company expects to enjoy future economic benefits from owning the asset

25. An investor is trying to understand goodwill in a company they plan to invest in. They ask the following questions:

Q1: What goodwill will they recognize when they acquire the company?

Q2: What goodwill should they expect in the company's stock price?

Which of the following responses will correctly answer the investor's question?

A. Q1 – Accounting goodwill. Q2 – Economic goodwill

B. Q1 – Economic goodwill. Q2 – Accounting goodwill

C. Q1 – Economic goodwill. Q2 – Both accounting and economic goodwill

The correct answer is A

From the understanding of goodwill, the following statements are true:

Economic goodwill: This goodwill is recognized from the company's performance in the economy. It is theoretical, and is not shown in the balance sheet. It is only expressed in the company's stock price.

Accounting goodwill: This goodwill is only recognized when you acquire the company. It is expressed under accounting standards.

26. Axe Capital has the following debt ratios:

Debt to equity ratio = 1.25

Total debt ratio = 40%

Determine Axe Capital's closest leverage ratio

A. 0.32

B. 3.13

C. 3.2

The correct answer is B

Financial leverage

= Total debt to equity ratio / Total debt ratio

= 1.25/0.4

=3.125

27. Bush Plantation Inc purchased an equipment for $5 million on 1st January, 2016. Their accounting policy is to depreciate assets on a straight-line method at 8%. For the sake of taxation, Bush Plantation has a policy of depreciating assets at 12% on a straight-line method.

On 1st January 2017, Bush Plantation revalued the equipment for $8 million, and reported that the machine will be in use for 20 years following the recent revaluation. For the sake of taxation, Bush

Plantation Inc accountants were advised not to recognize the revaluation.

The prevailing tax rate is 30% and the equipment is not expected to have a salvage value for the sake of taxation and financial reporting. Determine the deferred tax liability for Bush Plantation Inc as at 31st December, 2017.

A. $400,000

B. $120,000

C. $600,000

The correct answer is B

Accounting purpose depreciation

= 5 million x 8% = 400,000

Tax purpose depreciation

= 5 million x 12% = 600,000

31st December 2016, carrying amount

= 5 million – 400,000 = 4.6 million

31st December 2016 tax base

= 5 million – 600,000 = 4.4 million

Revaluation

= 8 million – 4.6 million = 3.4 million

31st December, 2017 carrying amount

= 8 million – (8 million / 20 years) = 7.6 million

31st December 2017 tax base

= 4.4 million – 600,000 = 3.8 million

Revaluation surplus reduction

= 3.4 million x 30% = 1.02 million

Deferred tax liability

= (7.6 million – 3.8 million) x 30% – 1.02 million

= $120,000

28. Your company purchased an equipment that is carried at $12,000. Upon estimation, the expected future cash flows from the equipment is $10,800, while the present value of the cash flows is $9,600. The fair value of the machine is reported as $9,000, the selling costs are estimated at $1000.
Using both the GAAP and IFRS standards, determine the impairment charge on the equipment
A. GAAP $2,400   IFRS $3,000
B. GAAP $3,000   IFRS $2,400
C. GAAP $ 2,400   IFRS $1,200
The correct answer is B
GAAP:
An impaired asset is one whose recoverable amount is less than the carrying value, which equals the total amount of undiscounted cash flows the company expects to derive from the asset.
Impairment loss
= 12,000 – 9,000
= $3,000
IFRS:
The recoverable amount is compared against the carrying amount to determine the higher of the fair value minus cost to sell.
Impairment loss
= 12,000 – 9,600
= $2,400
Chapter 5: Corporate Finance
Corporate governance refers to the management system that runs a company. In the shareholder theory, the company is run with the aim of

maximizing profits for shareholders. In the stakeholder theory, all the stakeholders to the company must participate in decision making. Creditors are interested in the ability of the company to meet its debt obligations, over company growth. Equity shareholders are interested in the long-term growth of the company. They look forward to dividends at the end of the trading period. Customers are more interested in the value proposition of the company when they pay for goods and services.

Stakeholder relationships can be affected by market and non-market factors. Market factors concern the capital markets, and can be handled through shareholder activism and annual meetings. Non-market factors like the legal requirements within the local jurisdiction can also affect the company.

The success of a company can also be affected by poor management. Without the right control mechanisms, some stakeholders can benefit at the expense of others, in the process exposing the company to reputational, regulatory, and legal risks including loss of business and penalties.

Companies must embrace an environmental, social, and governance analysis (ESG). This analysis examines all the factors that affect stakeholders, and helps you eliminate companies whose policies show weakness, when choosing potential investment options.

Capital Budgeting

Capital budgeting is about the prospect of the company for the future, especially on investments longer than a year. In capital budgeting, you consider the cost against the benefits of different projects to determine the best way of apportioning company resources to investments. Capital budgeting takes place in the following steps:

Identify projects with potential

Conduct an analysis on the projects, in terms of profitability and projected cash flow

Draft capital budget plans

Monitor and audit the project

Capital budgeting projects exist in different categories. Replacement projects are for replacing damaged or obsolete equipment with better, more efficient processes, machinery, and equipment. Expansion projects are for expanding the production or business capacity of the firm. New products are for expanding the products and service range. Regulatory, environmental and safety projects are aimed at meeting external requirements set by the government or regulators. Decisions around capital budgeting are structured on cash flows instead of accounting profits. Costs of financing are ignored in capital budgeting. Sunk costs do not affect future spending since they are already incurred.

Capital rationing is a situation where you don't have sufficient resources to invest in the projects, hence you have to determine the best possible project for your investment. Projects with a positive NPV or the largest NPV if comparing different projects, will increase the profitability of the entire company.

The payback period is the duration of time in years it takes to recoup the initial investment on a project. A discounted payback period is similar, but the future cash flows are discounted to determine the present value, hence determining the duration of time it will take to repay back the investment in the project.

Profitability index refers to the ratio of the discounted cash flow of a project against the original investment in the project. The greater the index, the more favorable it is as an indicator of a worthwhile investment.

Cost of Capital

Cost of capital refers to the price a company must pay to access the investment resources.

Successful companies should be able to earn more from operations and running projects than they can from sources of capital.

Weighted average cost of capital is the preferred metric, since companies might have different sources of capital. The more capital a company accumulates, the higher costs it is exposed to, and the higher risk of diminishing returns on different projects. It is wise, therefore, to make up for risk levels by adjusting capital assumptions.

To determine the cost of debt financing, you can either use the debt-rating approach or the yield-to-maturity approach. The latter expresses the present value of the future bond payments to the market price. The debt-rating approach, on the other hand, is applicable when you don't have information on the company debt, hence the use of relevant debt securities in the market.

Companies can also raise capital through preferred stock. Unlike common equity, preferred stocks carry different claims on the company ownership. Their dividend rates are higher, though they do not have voting rights. Companies can also raise money through common equity. To do this, the company can issue new stock, or reinvest earnings into its operations instead of paying out dividends. Shareholders in any of these methods will look forward to a specified rate of return, which is the cost of equity capital. This can be calculated in one of the following methods:

Capital asset pricing model (CAPM)

Cost of equity = Risk-free interest rate + Equity beta (Expected market return – Risk-free interest rate)

Dividend discount model

Cost of equity = (Dividend due in the proceeding period / Current share price) + Growth rate for the dividend

Bond yield plus risk premium method

Cost of equity = Bond yield + Equity risk premium

Measure of Leverage

Leverage is about uncertainty in the market. All companies hope to succeed in the foreseeable future, but investments and returns from operation are not always predictable. Through leverage, companies basically use more fixed costs in order to spur growth.

Leveraging carries the following risks:

Business risk – these are risks associated with the operational processes.

Financial risk – these are risks associated with the company's capital models (equity or debt).

Operating risk – these risks are associated with the operational structure in the company, and how fixed costs are used in production.

Sales risk – these are risks associated with the market, especially whether the company's prices and quantity of goods produced will succeed in the market.

The risks above can be quantified by using the following ratios:

Degree of operating leverage (DOL)

This ratio determines how sensitive the firm's operating income is to sales unpredictability. The formula is:

$$= Q(P - V) / \{Q(P - V) - F\}$$

Degree of financial leverage (DFL)

This ratio determines how sensitive the firm's operating income is to fluctuation in the earnings potential. The formula is:

$$= Q(P - V) - F / \{Q(P - V) - F - C\}$$

Degree of total leverage (DTL)

This ratio determines how sensitive the company's net income is to fluctuations in the number of units sold. It is basically a combination of DOL and DFL, and the formula is as follows:

$$= Q (P - V) / \{Q (P - V) - F - C\}$$

For the purpose of the formulas above, these representations apply:

Q – Quantity of units sold

P – Unit price of goods sold

F – Fixed cost for each unit sold

V – Variable cost of each unit sold

C – Cost of financing

It is important to remember that companies that use too much leverage exert a lot of pressure on their earnings, because most of their money is tied up in interest payments. Leverage, however, can be used well, and result in increased cash flows and earnings, especially in a company that is properly run and enjoying a good economic period.

Given these considerations, and given the fixed and variable operating cost structure, we can determine the company's breakeven point as follows:

Breakeven quantity = (Fixed cost + Financing cost) / (Unit price – Variable cost per unit)

In the event that the company has zero operating profits, the breakeven point is calculated as follows:

Breakeven quantity = Fixed cost / (Unit price – Variable cost per unit)

Managing Working Capital

Company operations are funded through different sources, primarily trade credit, credit lines, cash balances and cash flow management. Companies can also file for bankruptcy and reorganize their finances, or liquidate some assets to raise working capital.

The liquidity position of a company is determined by drags and pulls. A drag refers to items that hold up availability of funds, such as obsolete inventory or unclaimed receivables. Pulls, on the other hand, refers to a situation where the company has to spend before they earn anything from sales.

Quick ratio and current ratios are commonly used to determine the liquidity of a company. Managing liquidity is impossible without proper understanding of the cycles the company goes through. One of these is the operating cycle, which represents the number of receivable and inventory days, which explains how long it takes the company to turn raw materials into finished products and earn from their sales. The company should strive to have as short a lag between the operating cycles as possible, as this means they don't have to depend on external sources of finance to maintain operations.

Any surplus funds can be invested in the following short-term positions:

Discount basis yield

Bond equivalent yield

Money market yield

It is equally important to manage inventory properly, because insufficient inventory means less sales, but at the same time, excess inventory carries a risk of expiry, and the inventory holds up operating capital. The company's efficiency in turning over inventory can be determined by the turnover ratio.

Practice Questions and Answers

1. Which method are you most unlikely to use to determine the cost of debt for a company?

A. Pure-play

B. Debt rating

C. Yield to maturity

The correct answer is A

To determine the cost of equity for a company, you must first find the beta. The beta is derived from the pure-play approach

2. Jars Corp. is planning to raise $2 million through a bank acceptance agreement. The bank offers an all-inclusive 8% rate. What is the effective borrowing cost that Jars Corp. will pay?

A. 9,32%

B. 8.05%

C. 7.78%

The correct answer is B

The effective borrowing cost is calculated as follows:

= [(0.08 x 2,000,000 x 1/12) / (2,000,000 – {0.08 x 2,000,000 x 1/12})] x 12

= 13,333.33 / (1,986,666.67) x 12

=8.05%

3. The following statements describe the perception of dividends to shareholders. Which statement is most likely the correct one?

A. The market value of a shareholder's wealth is positively reflected by stock dividends

B. Stock dividends are liable to taxation

C. The shareholder's cost per share held reduces each time dividends are paid

The correct answer is C

The total cost is not affected by dividends. However, when dividends are paid, the cost for every share held by the shareholders reduces.

4. The information below was derived from the books of a trading company. Use it to determine the closest result to the company's operating cycle:

Purchases $15,000

Accounts payable $3,000

Accounts receivable $5,000

Closing stock $3,800

Credit sales $40,000

Cost of goods sold $18,000

A. 77 days

B. 123days

C. 45 days

The correct answer is B

Inventory days

= 3,800 / (18,000/365)

= 77.06 days

Receivable days

= 5,000 / (40,000/365)

= 45.63 days

Operating cycle

= 77.06 + 45.63

= 122.7 days

5. Sheers Inc. is planning a $600 million investment in a project. According to the directors, the NPV of

cash flows that the company can generate from the project should be $900 million. Currently, Sheers Inc has 7.5 million shares priced at $100 each. If Sheers Inc. goes ahead with this new investment, what will be their new share price?

A. $135
B. $140
C. $150

The correct answer is B

NPV of the project
= 900 – 600 = $300 million

Current market value
= 7.5 x 100 = $750 million

Market value of Sheers Inc. after undertaking the new project
= 750 + 300 = $1,050 million

The new share price
= 1,050 /7.5
= $140

6. A company's board decided to use cash to repurchase shares. Which of the following statements is true about the company?

A. The company's leverage increases, their assets do not change, and the shareholders' equity decreases

B. The company's leverage does not change, but the shareholders' equity and assets decrease

C. The company's leverage increases while the shareholders' equity and assets decrease

The correct answer is C

Financing share repurchases with cash increases the company's leverage, but ties up its assets and shareholders' equity, hence the assets and shareholders' equity will decrease

7. Which of the following would you use to determine the cost of debt if you cannot establish a reliable market price for a firm's debt?

A. Coupon rate for the bonds

B. Matrix pricing

C. The interest expense in the profit and loss account

The correct answer is B

In the event that you cannot determine a reliable market price for a firm's debt, it is advisable to use the current rates according to the expected bond rating if the firm is issuing a new bond. This pricing model is referred to as matrix pricing.

8. The following information is available about Kurt Corporation. Use it to determine the degree of operating leverage from 2017 to expected 2018.

	2017	Expected 2018
Sales		150,000
	160,000	
Number of units sold	1,500	1,600
Operating income	40,000	56,000
Cost of interest	13,000	13,000
Financing costs	10,000	10,000
Taxes	8,500	13,400
Net income	12,400	22,200

A. 3.84

B. 3.45

C. 6

The correct answer is C

Degree of operating leverage
= % Change in operating income / % Change in number of units sold

Operating income
= (56,000 − 40,000)/40,000
= 0.4

Number of units sold
= (1,600 − 1,500)/1,500
= 0.067

Degree of operating leverage = 0.4/0.067
= 6

9. Schafer Corporation has a 0.3 debt to equity ratio. Their target is to have a ratio of 0.4. The current risk-free rate is 6%, with the expected market return at 14%. The company is mulling over investing in a project with a 1.3 beta. Assuming the company has a cost of debt after tax for 8%, and the prevailing tax rate is 40%, what is the closest value of the WACC that the directors should use to evaluate the feasibility of the project?

A. 10%

B. 8%

C. 6.84%

The correct answer is B

Cost of equity
= 0.06 + 1.3 (0.14 − 0.06)
= 10.88%

WACC using the weight components
= (0.1088 x 1/1.40) + (0.08 x 0.4/1.4)

= 8%

10. Which of the following exposures is a project's beta highly unlikely to be exposed to?

A. Default risk

B. Financial risk

C. Business risk

The correct answer is A

Default risk applies when you are planning a bond investment. There is no relationship between the default risk and investment in a project.

11. A motorcycle company recently launched a new model into the market. As a result, sales of the older models declined as the new one picked up. This situation is an example of which of the following scenarios?

A. Sunk costs

B. Externalities

C. Opportunity cost

The correct answer is B

The scenario above is an example of sales cannibalization, which represents a negative externality in the market.

12. The company is looking at the prospect of investing in two projects, X and Y. From analysis, project X has a steep NPV profile compared to project Y. Which of the following statements represents the likelihood that the crossover points for the two projects will happen when the NPV is $5,000?

A. Project X has a higher IRR than project Y

B. Project Y receives more total cash inflows than project X

C. Most of the cash flows received in project X will be earned at a later stage in the life of the project.

The correct answer is C

Project X has a steeper NPV compared to project Y. This can only mean that project X has a lower IRR compared to project Y, hence its x-intercept is lower. Most of the cash flows for project X will be received at a later date. Project X also has a higher y-intercept compared to project Y, which is an indication of higher expected cash flows.

13. Which of the following situations is most likely to cause a drag on liquidity for a company?

A. When money is moving out of the company too fast

B. When the company's creditworthiness is terrible

C. When there's a delay in money coming into the company

The correct answer is C

Liquidity drag is most likely to happen in a situation where there are delays in getting cash flowing into the company.

Chapter 6: Portfolio Management

The main agenda behind portfolio management is to diversify investments to maximize returns. By diversification, you strive to avoid exposing your investment to too much risk, especially on one type of asset. Through diversification, you limit your risk exposure without reducing your expected returns on your investment.

There are two types of investors: individual investors and institutional investors. Individual investors could be a person or families, while institutional investors are professional organizations. Each of these types of investors has unique goals they seek from the investment market. Retirement savings plans for employees are managed as defined contribution or defined benefit plans. In defined contribution, the employers contribute to the fund regularly. The amount at the maturity of the fund depends on the market performance.

In defined benefit plans, on the other hand, the employer only offers a pre-defined financial benefit to the employee when they retire. Given this risk, it is in the best interest of the employer to ensure the fund is properly managed. Portfolio management is done in the following steps:

Planning

In this stage, you outline in the investment policy statement, objectives, risks, portfolio benchmark and anything else the client needs to know before investing.

Execution

You determine the perfect asset mix to allocate in each portfolio, with a view of their expected returns. You will also determine the right securities to include in each portfolio, and finally, purchase the securities and initiate the investment.

Feedback

After investment, you must keep an eye on the assets to ensure your exposure limit is not exceeded according to the agreement within the investment policy statement.

Other than investing in the markets by building a specific portfolio, you can also consider pooled investments like mutual funds. In such a fund, each investor is entitled to returns on a pro-rata basis on the value of the mutual fund.

Open ended funds allow investors to trade in their positions, and each time, the portfolio manager has to make adjustments accordingly. Close ended funds, on the other hand, do not allow investors to create new shares, nor are they allowed entry or exit into or out of the fund.

Money market funds are short-term debt markets, and are used as an alternative for keeping bank deposits. Investors can have their funds managed either as passive or active investments.

Portfolio Risk and Return

The primary reason for investing is to earn returns on whichever asset class you own. One of the most important returns you should know how to calculate is the holding period return. This refers to the total investment yield expressed as a percentage of your opening investment. The formula is as follows:

(Closing value – Opening value + Dividends) / Opening value

This formula gives you the holding period return for one trading period. In case you have more than one period, you have to calculate the returns for each of them, then get their arithmetic mean. You can also use the geometric mean to calculate the average holding period return.

In case you need to determine and compare the returns for different periods, especially if their lengths are varied, you can use the annualized return calculation. In an annualized return, you simply compound the return by how long the period in question takes to form a year. In the case of a quarterly return, for example, you have to compound it four times as shown in the example below:

Annualized 9% quarterly return = $(1 + 0.09)^4 - 1 = 41.2\%$

Portfolio return is another measure that combines the return averages of all the securities in your portfolio. Most questions will present the portfolio contents, then you will be required to determine the portfolio return. To do this, multiply each security by its portfolio weight, then sum the results.

Remember that every investor considers risk in different ways. A risk seeker is an investor who is willing to accept risk, even if the likelihood of high returns is not expressly assured. A risk neutral investor is one who takes risk only when they are assured of a relevant return. A risk averse investor is one who tries to avoid risk by all means, and will gladly contend with a low return. Risk tolerance refers to an investor's willingness to accept risk.

Portfolio Planning and Construction

The capital market line (CML) is an approach that has been used by many investors in the past to determine their risk tolerance in an investment. Investors can take on different risk classes: systematic and unsystematic risk. A systematic risk is one that applies to all the investment markets. It includes things like political instability and the prevailing business cycle.

Non-systematic risk is a risk that only affects some assets. To diversify against such a risk, investors buy assets that do not have negative correlations, or those that have a very low correlation. There are different methods you can use to determine the expected return from a given portfolio. The simplest method is the multi-factor model. In this method, several inputs are added to determine the returns. Some of the factors you can consider include statistical or macroeconomic functions.

The three-factor method, which was further expanded to a four-factor method, considers the market beta, book-to-market value of the company, the size of the company and the security's momentum.

Of all these methods, the simplest is the single factor model. This model considers returns as a function of market exposure. Return in this model is determined as follows:

= Risk-free rate (1 – Beta) + Market return Beta

It is from this function that the multiple factor models are built, adding more factors and their respective betas accordingly.

As an investment banker, or advisor, it is important to ensure that the investor understands what you are working on, and your objectives align. All the important information they need prior to making an investment is contained in the investment policy statement. The following are the contents of an investment policy statement:

Introductory description of the prospective client.
Clear purpose statement.
Definition of duties and responsibilities of all parties to the investment.
Procedure to follow in updating the policy.
The investor's objectives and constraints
Review and evaluation protocols.

In as far as the portfolio is concerned, the important components of the policy statement are the objectives and constraints. This is where the investor learns about the risk and return, and it makes them psychologically prepared.

Risk Management

When managing an investment portfolio, risk management is one of the most important factors you must understand. For individual investors, risk management is unstructured and informal. In the case of institutional investors, however, risk management is well-structured, and involves understanding operational risks.

Risk governance encompasses policies and structures that outline performance all through the company. Risk identification and measurement refers to a process of monitoring and tracking identified risk exposures. Risk infrastructure refers to all the systems in place, including people, who conduct risk management on behalf of the company.

Processes and policies outline the guidelines under which the normal operations of the business can take place. Communication is an important part of risk management so that all the interested parties stay abreast with everything that's going on.

A risk management framework is important for any company because it helps them identify potential risks and prevent unnecessary surprises, enhances decision making and discipline, while at the same time limiting the risk of operational errors.

Fintech in Investment Management

Fintech is a term commonly used to refer to a combination of financial and technological matters. Fintech is advancing and currently includes machine learning technologies in making logical decisions.

Companies currently rely on different sources of data to make decisions. This can be obtained from the normal sources, like reports on the stock markets, or new methods like data obtained from electronic devices and social networks, and presented in a structured or unstructured approach. Computer systems have been developed that can make logical decisions through artificial intelligence. These systems greatly rely on machine learning languages either through supervised or unsupervised learning.

The use of fintech in investment management is a step in the right direction, because of the development of applications and programs that can read and understand complex algorithms and integrate them into the buy/sell decisions for account managers. These programs can also be built for automatic trading by monitoring the markets and executing trades where they foresee the possibility of good returns.

Practice Questions and Answers

1. The following terms are used to define tolerable risk. Which of the terms identifies tolerable risk based on unique metrics?

A. Risk budgeting
B. Enterprise risk management
C. Risk tolerance

The correct answer is A

Risk tolerance is a measure of an investor's risk appetite, which determines the level of risk that is acceptable to the investor. Risk budgeting is a measure and allocation of tolerable risk according to unique characteristics. It helps to determine how the investor takes risk.

2. In order to enjoy gains in the short-term, a portfolio manager may decide to make a temporary deviation from the strategic asset allocation of a given portfolio. This process is referred to as:

A. Portfolio reconstruction
B. Tactical asset allocation
C. Risk budgeting

The correct answer is B

In light of possible positive returns, a portfolio manager can set aside the set strategic asset allocation and deliberately deviate from the norm. This approach is tactical asset allocation.

3. Different investment vehicles have unique duration plans for their investment portfolios. Of the following three, which one is the least unlikely to have the shortest duration?

A. Foundations

B. Pension fund plans

C. Banks

The correct answer is C

The investment horizon for foundations and pension fund plans are generally long term. Banks, on the other hand, often make investments in shorter term horizons.

4. As a financial advisor, you meet an investor whose willingness to embrace risk is below average, but their ability to take risk is above average. How would you define this investor's risk tolerance?

A. The investor has average risk tolerance

B. The investor has below average risk tolerance

C. The investor has an above average risk tolerance

The correct answer is B

Investors who have an above average ability to take risks in their investments, but are unwilling to take the risk have a below average risk tolerance.

5. In a portfolio, what is the slope of a characteristic line least unlikely to represent?

A. Portfolio beta

B. Portfolio unsystematic risk

C. Portfolio total risk

The correct answer is A

We get the characteristic line when the returns of a given portfolio are regressed against market return at a specific point in time. Because of this reason, the slope of the characteristic line will represent the portfolio beta.

6. An investor's financial reports indicate that he earned – 0.8% returns by correctly predicting the movement of the yen/dollar exchange rate between 1st June 2018 to 7th June 2018. How much loss will the investor's account reflect by the end of the month?

A. 2.86%

B. 34.14%

C. 23.65%

The correct answer is B

Annualized investor return

$= (1 – 0.8\%)52 – 1$

$= -34.14\%$

7. The following statements reflect an investor's decisions given their risk profile. Which statement is the least unlikely of the investor?

S1 –An investor with a less risk averse profile does not have a steeper indifference curve compared to an investor with a more risk averse profile.

S2 – In the event of a negative correlation between a risk averse investor's portfolio and Asset X, the investor has a better chance of investing part of their portfolio in Asset X for a better risk-return tradeoff, as it is riskier than the investor's current portfolio.

A. S1 is true

B. S1 and S2 are true

C. S1 and S2 are untrue

The correct answer is B

Given an asset-portfolio correlation of less than 1, a risk averse investor is better off earning a good tradeoff if they invest part of their portfolio into a riskier asset.

8. Shantell is managing a hedge fund at Oakley Capital. She recently went long on equities whose values she expected to increase in the near future, and sold short on equities whose values she expected to decrease in value. Which of the following strategies is Shantell using?

A. Long/short strategy

B. Event driven strategy

C. Equity market neutral strategy

The correct answer is A

Shantell is using the long/short strategy. This is a strategy where the investment manager seeks profits from movements in the market instead of searching for equities that are either undervalued or overvalued.

9. The following statements describe a two-fund separation theorem. Which of the statements is the most unlikely to be true?

A. An investment decision can be made independent of the investor's tastes and preferences

B. One of the financial decisions you have to make is choosing an optimal portfolio.

C. The amount of money an investor is willing to invest depends on their level of risk preference.

The correct answer is B

The act of choosing the perfect portfolio is an investment decision, not a financial decision. The only financial decision being made should be determining the appropriate weight of the selected portfolio, at a risk-free rate.

10. The following statements describe an investment portfolio. Which of the statements is least unlikely?

S1 – If an investor has a negative coefficient in risk aversion, their indifference curve will have a negative slope.

S2 – It is possible to have a negative or positive weight for a risk-free asset if the portfolio has a minimum variance frontier.

A. All the statements are true

B. All the statements are untrue

C. Only one statement is true

The correct answer is C

In investment, utility increases as risk and return increase. For this reason, a risk-averse investor would have a negative slope on the indifference curve. Therefore, they have a negative coefficient in risk aversion.

Portfolios on the minimum variance frontier would only contain very risky assets, with zero weight.

11. An investor's decision to allocate assets is affected by specific needs and preferences. Which of the following statements refers to the least unlikely example of such preferences?

A. The decision to avoid investment with companies that contribute to environmental degradation and pollution.

B. The decision to invest in municipal securities in order to take advantage of their tax exemption status.

C. The decision to invest at least 12% of the investor's portfolio in cash investments

The correct answer is A

An investor's unique perception of an investment or company based on their social or personal concessions might make it difficult for them to invest in some companies, excluding them from their portfolio, regardless of the potential for good returns.

12. You come across an investment portfolio that has a low total return compared to the market portfolio, but it also has a high total risk. Which of the following statements is the most unlikely reference to this portfolio?

A. The portfolio cannot lie on the security market line

B. The portfolio carries a very high unsystematic risk

C. The portfolio's beta is less than 1

The correct answer is A

In the event that a portfolio carries unsystematic risk, but most of that risk can be diversified away, the underlying portfolio can lie on the security market line. In order to plot on the security market line, the beta for the portfolio must be less than 1 because the market portfolio return is higher than the portfolio's expected return.

13. The following information is available about a stock in the market:

Risk premium in the equity market = 6%

Risk-free rate = 4%

Beta 0.6

Current market price = $48

Expected market price at the end of the year= $52

Expected dividends at the end of the year = $4

Based on this information, what would you conclude about the value of the stock?

A. The stock is overvalued

B. The stock is undervalued

C. The stock's valuation is correct

The correct answer is B

Expected rate of return

$= (52 - 48 + 4) / 48$

$= 16.67\%$

Required rate of return

$= 0.04 + 0.6 (0.06)$

$= 7.6\%$

Since the required rate of return is lower than the expected rate of return, this stock is undervalued.

14. Parents set up an investment trust on behalf of their infant with strict rules that they would only use the trust to buy their first house. Which of the constraints below is most unlikely concerning the investment trust?

A. Occurrence of unique circumstances

B. Liquidity constraints

C. Tax liability concerns

The correct answer is B

The investment trust is not expected to have a liability concern for a very long time, given that it is impossible that the infant will draw funds from their trust until they are old enough to buy their first house.

15. The following statements refer to good risk governance practices that should be implemented in a company:

S1 – Allow for the implementation of a risk management committee

S2 – Provide the company management with clear guidance

S3 – Create room for the appointment of a chief risk officer

S4 – Emphasize on enterprise risk management

A. All the statements are true

B. All the statements are true, but S4

C. All the statements are true, but S1

The correct answer is C

A company that practices good risk governance should focus on enterprise risk management, meaning that the entire company's risk is governed.

In light of this, the company must make sure the right governance structures are put in place, including hiring a chief risk officer, or establishing a risk forum.

A good risk governance framework will also have measures in place to guide the management, while at the same time allowing them room to execute their mandate in light of the business objectives and strategies.

Chapter 7: Equity

There are different reasons why investors choose financial markets. There are six activity levels, however, that attract different investors.

Organizations and individuals trade in investment markets for savings so that their money and assets can grow over time. Entities that do not have sufficient funds for their operations can borrow and repay in the future.

Registered companies sell ownership in their entities in the form of shares, which is a way of raising equity capital, in exchange for cash immediately. Futures and forwards are derivative securities that are used for risk management.

In the spot market trading, investors can exchange currency for another currency or another item. Equity markets are full of information motivated traders. These are investors who pursue information advantages to purchase securities below their value and benefit when the values of the securities rise in the future.

There are different assets that are traded in the securities market. Equity and debt securities are the most popular because they attract a lot of attention even from the general public. Commodities are items that do not have a trade use, but are still traded in the market, such as agricultural produce. Governments issue currencies, investors agree on contracts to trade their assets in the future.

Security Market Indices

An index in the security market represents an asset class or a specific segment in the security market. These indices enable investors to monitor the performance of specific assets. The indices act as benchmarks against which index funds and investment funds are tracked. The formula for determining the price return index is given as follows:

Value of index = (The aggregate of the number of units in the index x The price of securities in the index) / The index divisor

$V = (nP)/D$

The following steps will guide you when building a proper index:

Determine the broadness or narrowness of the target market

Choose the right securities within the target market

Establish the weight of each security in the index

Determine how regularly you will need to rebalance the index to maintain its exposure

There are different weighting methods that you can use, depending on your preference as they all have unique strengths and weaknesses. Equal weighting diversifies the portfolio's exposure, but must be rebalanced frequently. Price weighting is the easiest method, but it uses arbitrary weights. Indices must be adjusted regularly in order to maintain consistency in their exposure. This is done through rebalancing. Reconstruction refers to a situation where you change the securities in the index. It is a good option in case some of the securities in the index are no longer in line with the set criteria, or if you come across new securities that meet the desired criteria.

There are different roles that indices play in the financial markets. They help you determine the public perception of the market because people usually monitor the rise and fall regularly. They are, therefore, good benchmarks for an investment manager, and can be helpful when used as model portfolios for a passive fund.

Popular indices include the broad market, style, sector, and multi-market indices. There are different types of fixed income indices, and they are often grouped according to the issuer's maturity, payment currency, geolocation, economic sector, quality of credit or any other characteristics unique to the issue. It is also possible to identify special fixed income indices like inflation-linked indices, high yield indices and emerging market indices.

Market Efficiency

Market efficiency refers to the manner in which new information is absorbed and reflected in the market prices for investments. In an efficient market, the market prices immediately respond to new information, and because of this reason, it is almost impossible to outperform the market or if you do, it is impossible to sustain it for the long run. Active managers thrive in an inefficient market because they are able to outperform the market by staying ahead of everyone in information access.

The market price of a security refers to the price at which that security can be purchased or sold. The intrinsic value of a security, on the other hand, is the value that investors place on the security in question if they come to understand what the asset's true features are.

Efficiency in a market is determined by a lot of factors. One of these is the number of participants in the market and the level of sophistication. The market is more efficient if more sophisticated participants are available. This is also hugely reliant on the ease of access to information. Limited access to information means that the market will have a lot of inefficiencies. Market efficiency can also be hindered when sanctions on trading activities are imposed.

Market efficiency can either be:

Weak – All historical information is included in the security prices.

Semi-strong – Only publicly available information is available in the prices. Investors are unable to enjoy supernatural profits using public information. Strong – Private and public information is reflected in security prices.

Based on these classifications, investors can earn significant returns by engaging in active management, insider trading, fundamental analysis and technical analysis.

A market anomaly is an exception to the fundamental concept of market efficiency. This is the occurrence of an action that might not be associated to any of the usual information available in the markets.

Anomalies include the time series effect like the January effect, and cross sectional anomalies like the size effect where large companies perform poorer than smaller companies. The understanding of market efficiency is influenced by the fundamentals of behavioral finance. While conventional finance demands that participants in the market be rational investors, this is not always the case.

Equity Securities

Equity securities are an investor's claim on the company's ownership rights and assets. They allow an investor rights like the right to vote on matters concerning the company. There are different types of shares. Common shares allow the investor common ownership interest. They can vote on most of the issues affecting the company, and elect members to the board. Preferred shares enjoy preferential treatment, especially on dividend allocation, and claims to the company assets. However, they lack voting rights

A company's shares can be private or public, depending on whether the company makes them available to the public. While private companies stock markets are generally smaller than the public stock market, there has been an increase in the number of companies venturing in this sector in recent years.

Public companies endure more scrutiny. Their securities are easier to purchase in secondary markets and they are more liquid. Private securities, on the other hand, are frequently traded through trade negotiations between the inherent investors.

Thanks to technological advancement, it is now easier for investors to trade in securities in markets from all over the world. If you want to invest beyond the limits of your country, there are several options you can consider, including direct investment, depository receipts, and global registered shares.

Equity securities deliver returns in the form of dividend income and capital appreciation. Preference shareholders typically earn more returns from dividends as long as they hold onto their shareholding. The returns are arrived at as follows:

$Rt = (Pt - Pt - 1 + Dt) / Pt - 1$

In the formula above, Rt refers to the total return, P refers to the sale price, Pt – 1 refers to the purchase price, while Dt refers to the expected dividend income.

The primary aim of issuing securities is to raise capital for the company to invest or to fund their operations. Such capital is often used to cultivate the company's value, in the process maximizing on the long-term wealth of shareholders, and growing the value of the company through distributed dividends.

The company's equity value, on the other hand, is determined by the market value of the company or its book value. Book value refers to a historical overview of the financing and operating decisions of management. Market value refers to an assessment of the company by investors, based on their expectation of the future cash flow in the company from its operations. Companies that have a high price to book ratio have very high growth expectations in the market. A high price to book ratio refers to a company whose market price is relatively high in relation to the book value.

Industry and Company Analysis

Industry analysis is an investor's understanding of the company they invest in, and the business environment in which the company is operating. This information is used by analysts to determine the best equity investments, and how certain factors will affect their investment strategy, or their portfolio selection. An industry is a group of companies that share some similar characteristics. They can be classified according to the cyclical nature of their operations, the type of goods or services they offer, or similarities in their historical return statistics.

Industries can also be classified under the following systems:

Global Industry Classification Standard

Russel Global Sectors

Industry Classification Benchmark

The sensitivity of a company to business and economic cycles can be used to sort companies. Cyclical companies, for example, experience highly volatile growth and returns. It is important for an analyst to understand the difference between different companies in different industries, and how these differences affect their performance, hence their impact if included in a given portfolio.

To be thorough in your analysis, you must identify the life cycle of an industry, the important segments in the industry, and the economic forces that have a significant impact on the operations of companies in that industry. In light of this, Michael Porter identified the following five forces for strategic company and industrial analysis:

Threat of substitutes

Threat of entry

Buyer power

Supplier power

Competition among existing participants

Barrier to entry influences the profitability of an industry, because more barriers keep the existing profit margins high for the existing companies. Fewer barriers to entry open up the industry to more firms, which increases competition, and over time the participating firms are unable to sustain their market share.

The life cycle of an industry has five stages:

Embryonic stage – low sales volumes, high prices and lethargic growth

Growth stage – increased productivity, increased demand, low competition

Shakeout stage – increased competition, reduced profitability, slowing growth

Maturity stage – very little growth, high entry barriers, consolidation among participating firms

Decline stage – negative growth, intense competition, excess production

The growth of an industry can be influenced by a number of external factors. These include structural and cyclical macroeconomic trends, profitability from the cost of accessing money, and changing consumer behavior. Some industries are exposed to radical changes in light of technological advancement, which might involve reinventing their business models.

When analyzing a company, your analysis will only be complete if it includes an explanation of the company's pricing environment, the product or service demand and supply analysis, important financial ratios, overview of operations, trends and characteristics of the company.

Equity Valuation

If the market price of an equity security is equal to its value estimate, the security is considered to be fairly valued. Security valuation is affected by a lot of uncertainty, and this can determine whether the market value is lower or higher than the estimated company value.

Equity securities can be valued using the following models:

Asset-based valuation

Discounted cash flow

Market multiple models

In discounted cash flow models, the concept is to determine the present value of expected future cash flows to the investment. The dividend discount model is one such example, which is preferred by mature companies. The formula is as follows:

Present value = $D_t / (1 + r)t + P_n / (1 + r)n$

In the formula above, D_t represents the dividends at a given time, P_n represents the anticipated selling price at a given time, while r represents the required rate of return.

The free cash flow to equity model is another discounted cash flow method used in equity securities. It is used to determine the present value of future cash flows that can be shared as dividends.

Market multiple models can be used to establish a company's value by developing a calculated value about the company from market valuation information and available accounting information about the company.

Asset based valuation depends on the fair market value of the company's assets and liabilities. Most companies that use this method have a high portion of marketable current assets and very few intangible assets. This is because of the difficulty in determining the value of intangible assets. Besides, the book value of intangible assets might be inaccurate or irrelevant to an investor. Since this valuation method does not consider the growth rate of the company, earnings or anticipated cash flows, it is one of the easiest methods because there is no need for assuming projections. That being said, they are not the best methods for determining the value of a company operating as a going concern, unless they are used alongside other models.

Practice Questions and Answers

1. You are planning to short sell a security, but realize that it is very difficult to borrow. Given this situation, what would be the best description of the short rebate rate for this security?

A. The short rebate rate is very low or negative

B. The short rebate rate is very high

C. The short rebate rate is higher than the overnight rate by 10 basis points

The correct answer is A

Securities that are very difficult to borrow for short selling are usually special. Their rebate rates are either negative or very low. If this were not the case, they usually have a rebate rate that is lower than the overnight interbank funds market rate by 10 basis points.

2. In which valuation model does the EV/EBITDA metric apply as a common input?

A. Asset-based valuation model

B. Multiplier model

C. Present value model

The correct answer is B

EV/EBITDA stands for enterprise value on earnings before interest, tax depreciation and amortization, and it is frequently applied in multiplier models.

3. When conducting a security valuation using the top-down method, which of the following steps is usually the last one?

A. Company analysis

B. Economy analysis

C. Industry analysis

The correct answer is A

The company analysis is the last step in security valuation following the top-down method.

4. The statements below describe the fundamental weighting method. Which of the statements is the least unlikely to be true?

A. The fundamental weighting method is biased in favor of the highest value stocks because they are apportioned the highest weight in any index.

B. The fundamental weighting method is similar to the momentum investment strategy because as the relative investment values increase, the security weights reduce.

C. The fundamental weighting method is unbiased around shares of companies that have very large market capitalization.

The correct answer is B

Statement A and C are false. Like the contrarian investment strategy, the weight of securities whose relative values increase are reduced, while the opposite is true for the securities whose relative values increase, in the fundamental weighting method. The fundamental weighting method is also unbiased towards shares of companies that have a large market capitalization

5. When are holders of put option common shares least unlikely to exercise their right?

A. When the prevailing market price is lower than the exercise price

B. When the intrinsic value of the stock is lower than the exercise price

C. When the intrinsic value of the stock is higher than the exercise price

The correct answer is A

Investors who hold put option common shares are willing to sell their shares back to the company in the event that the exercise price is higher than the stock price.

6. Investors in Aristos Inc recently received their annual dividends. The company's shares are trading on a 20.7 P/E ratio. It is expected that the company will pay dividends worth $18.56 in the following year. Analysts also believe the dividends paid will indefinitely grow at a rate of 4.2%.

Assuming that the stock is currently trading at $465.23, which is the closest market required rate of return for the stock?

A. 8.98%

B. 8.19%

C. 10.32%

The correct answer is B

Cost of equity using the Gordon growth DDM

= (18.56 / 465.23) + 4.2%

= 8.19%

7. The following statements describe different industry classification systems. Which of the statements is the least unlikely to be true?

Statement 1 – Commercial industry classification systems cannot differentiate non-profit from profit taking organizations.

Statement 2 – Commercial industry classification systems are not updated or reviewed as regularly as government industry classification systems.

A. Both statements are untrue

B. Statement 1 is true

C. Statement 2 is true

The correct answer is A

Government industry classification systems do not differentiate between non-profit and profit taking organizations.

Government industry classification systems are actually updated and reviewed less frequently than commercial industry classification systems.

8. You own 750 shares in a local company. The company is planning to call a vote where the

shareholders will elect 8 new directors. In light of statutory voting, how can you vote for your preferred directors?

A. You can place a maximum of 750 votes for each of your preferred candidates

B. You can place 6,000 votes and share them in whichever proportion you wish for your preferred candidates.

C. You can only place 750 votes for your preferred candidates

The correct answer is B

According to statutory voting, each share you own entitles you to one voting right. Therefore, you can cast no more than 750 votes for each of your preferred candidates. You are at liberty to share the voting rights to your candidates in whichever way you please.

9. In a recent announcement, Henkel Industries indicated they will not be paying dividends for the next four years. From the fifth year, they will pay dividends at a payout ratio of 40%. Projections indicate the company's earnings per share in the fourth year will be $8.20, and it has an 8.5% growth potential forever. If the cost of equity is 15%, what is the current value of Henkel Industries' stock?

A. $32.30

B. $31.67

C. $54.75

The correct answer is A

Earnings per share in the 5th year

$= 8.20 \times 1.085 = 8.897$

Dividends in the 5th year

$= 8.897 \times 0.4 = 3.5588$

Price at the end of the 4th year

$= 3.5588 / (0.15 - 0.085) = 54.75$

Current value of Henkel Industries stock

$= 54.75 / (1.15)4$

$= \$31.30$

10. The following statements are true about three companies, X, Y and Z. Company X is in the gold mining business, and their reserves are known. Company Y is a struggling internet provider that is currently under liquidation. Company Z is in the hotel industry, and has grown in size over the years by acquiring small hotel chains.

Asset-based valuation was used to determine the value of these companies. In which company is this approach inappropriate?

A. Company X

B. Company Y

C. Company Z

The correct answer is C

Using asset-based valuation is only recommended in a scenario where it is possible to reliably determine the company's assets and liabilities, especially when the company does not have many intangible assets.

Company Z has acquired a lot of small hotels. Therefore, it enjoys immense goodwill in the form of internally generated goodwill and acquired goodwill. Because of this reason, asset-based valuation is not appropriate for Company Z.

11. Gregor Corp shares are thinly traded at the exchange. An investor places a market purchase order for these shares. What is the main challenge that the investor should expect from their new investment?

A. This is a very expensive trade to execute.

B. This is a very difficult trade to execute

C. This purchase order will be fulfilled, but at a very low price.

The correct answer is A

Market orders involve two decisions. When an investor places an order, other investors in the market are probably placing an order for the opposite side. Because of this reason, market orders are generally executed immediately.

However, in the case of a market for thinly traded shares, executing orders can be very expensive. This also happens in a case where the order placed is very large, in relation to the current trading activity in the market. When this happens, the only way these orders can be fulfilled is at very high prices.

12. Of the following industries, which is the most unlikely to be concentrated when trading at global level?

A. Branded pharmaceuticals

B. Oil and related services

C. Candy and confectionery

The correct answer is B

There are very few companies that have been able to provide a complete range of services in the oil industry. These are companies that have major financial backing, and in most cases, they are backed by the governments in their jurisdiction. However, at the same time there are many small companies that operate in the oil and related service industry. These small firms specialize in specific services within the oil industry. This also explains why national oil companies and their service agencies usually control a large market share in the countries of operation.

13. The following statements concern Porter's five forces framework. Which statement is not true?

A. Threat of substitutes

B. Macroeconomic influence

C. Threat of new entrants

The correct answer is B

Porter's five forces are as follows:

Intense rivalry

Threat of new entrants in the market

Supplier bargaining power

Consumer bargaining power

Threat of substitutes

14. What is the possible explanation for the difference in performance of underlying commodities and the commodity indices in the market?

A. There is limited information transparency, and as a result, commodity indices largely trade as illiquid instruments

B. There are many factors that determine the possible returns for commodity indices

C. The returns for commodity indices are less volatile than returns for the commodities

The correct answer is B

The following explanations are true for the difference in performance of commodity indices and the underlying commodities:

Returns on the commodity indices take into consideration the roll yield, collateral return and the returns from any price fluctuations in the future.

Instead of basing the value of indices on the value of the real commodities, they are based on future contracts.

15. The market indices below should be rebalanced from time to time. Which of the three is the least unlikely to be rebalanced regularly?

A. Market cap weighted indices

B. Price weighted indices

C. Equal weighted indices

The correct answer is C

It is imperative that equal weighted indices are rebalanced regularly as soon as there are fluctuations in the prices of the underlying securities.

16. A large private equity firm invests in public companies by purchasing them at very good discount rates and using their position to gain influence over the companies' business operations. Which kind of private equity investors would be most likely attracted to the private equity firm?

A. Private investment in public equity fund

B. Leverage buyout fund

C. Management buyout fund

The correct answer is A

A private investment in public equity fund refers to a private equity investment vehicle that targets public companies that are in need of sizeable capital funding to finance their business operations. Such investors look for companies that can willingly cede a significant part of their ownership to the new investors, by selling to them at a discount rate in relation to the present market value.

17. An investor wishes to purchase shares in Hocks Corporation, with a view to the following dividend allocation over the next three years:

Year 1 $20.00 per share

Year 2 $22.00 per share

Year 3 $24.00 per share

In three years, the investor wishes to sell his shares for $408 per share, and is looking forward to a 14% internal rate of return per annum if they invest in this company. Hocks Corporation shares are currently trading in the market at $346 per share. Which of the following statements represents the investor's correct assessment of the stock at the moment?

A. The stock is overvalued

B. The stock is fairly valued

C. The stock is undervalued

The correct answer is A

To determine the value of the company's stock, the investor must discount the expected cash flows as follows:

= 20 / (1 + 14%)1 + 22 / (1 + 14%)2 + 24 / (1 + 14%)3 + 408 / (1 + 14%)3

= 17.544 + 16.928 + 16.199 + 275.388

= $326.059 per share

The investor is right to believe the shares of the company are overvalued

18. The following information is available about an equity market security from multiple dealers in the industry. What is the bid-ask spread?

Bid $44.95   Ask $45.65

Bid $45.25   Ask $45.85

Bid $45.15   Ask $45.50

A. $0.95

B. $0.25

C. $0.55

The correct answer is B

The best bid price in the market = 45.25

The best ask price in the market = 45.50

The market bid-ask spread = 45.50 – 45.25 = $0.25

19. The margin account balance for your investment has dropped below the maintenance margin. You will be called upon to restore which of the following?

A. Maintenance margin

B. Variation margin

C. Initial margin

The correct answer is A

If the maintenance margin is higher than your equity margin account, you are expected to fund the account with an amount sufficient to restore the account maintenance margin.

20. The growth of an industry is affected by microeconomic and macroeconomic factors, among other things. Which of the factors listed below is the most unlikely macroeconomic variable that can influence an economy?

A. GDP

B. Technological advancement

C. Availability of credit

The correct answer is B

The growth of an industry, its profits and revenue is influenced by the following factors:

Social influences

Government initiatives

Demographic influences

Macroeconomic influences

Technological influences

The macroeconomic variables that are responsible for influencing industrial growth are availability of credit, inflation, GDP, and interest rates.

Chapter 8: Fixed Income

Bonds are debt instruments that guarantee buyers cash flow in the future. They can be issued by governments, companies, or organizations like the EU. There are three types of bonds:

Structured bonds

Corporate bonds

Government bonds

Bonds are also identified by their credit risk.

Investment grade bonds are high quality with lower

risk and low yields. High-yield or junk bonds are riskier and have a very high likelihood of default. An indenture is a legal document that outlines the terms and conditions of a specific bond agreement, like the frequency, coupon rate, and face value. To reduce the risk in a bond, they might include some credit additions, like insurance.

Bonds are domiciled according to the issuer's jurisdiction. Domestic bonds are issued in the country of origin, while foreign bonds are issued in a different country from the issuer's domicile.

The structure of a bond includes periodic interest payments (coupons), and a principal payment when the term matures. Fixed coupon rates are consistent through the term of the bond, while floating coupon rates are variable against a unique benchmark.

Bonds can also have contingency arrangements which bestow unique rights to the issuer and the holder, like call and put options, which give the subject the right but not the obligation to purchase or sell the bond at a given date in the future. A convertible bond is a unique blend of equity and debt security. In special circumstances, the bondholder can convert the bond to equity shares.

Fixed Income Markets

London Interbank Offered Rate (LIBOR) is the most common benchmark upon which floating rates are determined. Just like in equity security markets, the bond market has primary and secondary markets. In primary markets, an underwritten offering allows bond purchase after negotiating the price. Syndicated offerings involve large bond offerings that have to be undertaken by several underwriters. In secondary markets, you can purchase bonds over the counter (OTC) or at an exchange.

The bid-ask spread is the difference between the market bid and ask quotes for the security. The spread indicates how liquid the security is. A large spread means the security is illiquid.

Bond issues that mature in less than one year are referred to as T-bills. They are issued at a lower price than their face value. T-bonds and T-notes have longer maturities compared to T-bills, and they are often issued at face value.

Governments are also involved in issuing other unique bonds which are neither government nor corporate. One example is a non-sovereign bond. It is issued to fund public development projects, but the national government does not guarantee it. Non-sovereign bonds have very high yields, and low default rates.

Quasi-government bonds are not guaranteed by the government, but are backed by the government. Supranational bonds are issued by organizations like the EU and the IMF.

Debt is a financing tool used by companies to raise funds for different projects and investments. Commercial papers are used to solicit short-term financial support. The debt agreement matures in less than 90 days.

Banks can raise funds by borrowing from the central bank or other local banks, with loan agreements of less than a year. They can also use certificates of deposit, offering depositors relatively high rates for fixed deposit amounts.

A repurchase agreement (repo) is a unique lending vehicle where a financial market security is sold, backed by an agreement to purchase it in the future at a predetermined price. The underlying asset in the agreement is usually the collateral, so repurchase agreements are naturally collateralized contracts.

Fixed Income Valuation

The value of a bond issue is represented by its present value, and the expected value of cash flows in the future. While future equity security cash flows are largely undefined, bond cash flows are predetermined. The investor is aware of when they expect payment and how much, at the time they sign the bond agreement.

The discount rate is determined by the market rate. With this in mind, the value of the bond falls as the market rate rises. If the coupon rate is higher than the market rate, the bond trades at a premium. The yield to maturity for bonds refers to the internal rate of return that equates the prevailing price of the bond to the present value of future cash flows.

Fluctuations in the value of a bond are determined by different factors. Here are some examples:

Inverse effect – the bond price moves in the opposite direction to interest rates

Convexity effect – expect a lower change in the percentage bond price for interest rate increases than decreases.

Coupon effect – high coupon bonds have a lower percentage price change compared to low coupon bonds when interest rates fluctuate

Maturity effect

You can use spot rates to determine the present value of a bond by using a different discount rate for every cash flow period. Given the unique nature of interest accruals, bond prices are quoted either as the flat price or the full price.

Pay attention to the day counting method used when calculating the time elapsed since the last bond payment. Time elapsed is calculated either as 30/360 or actual-actual method. In the 30/360 method, we assume that each month has 30 days, and 360 days in the year. In the actual-actual method, you use the calendar days for that specific year.

A yield curve is a graph that represents a given security over a range of maturities. The curve slopes upwards because lengthy maturity periods have higher returns. You will notice the curve flattening for longer maturity periods because the difference in returns reduces. A spot curve displays the spot rates for every maturity period. On the other hand, a par curve displays the yield to maturity for par value bonds.

You can quote bond rates as spot or forward rates. Spot rates are determined immediately, while forward rates are used in the future. An implied forward rate is a bond whose rate is determined according to the spot rate.

Asset-backed Securities

An asset backed security is different from bonds, because while bonds might be backed by the money lent to the bond issuer which has to be paid back at a predetermined time, asset backed securities are based on asset classes that are grouped together as collateral to become a fixed income security. Assets in this kind of arrangement are managed by special purpose entities (SPEs). The assets are classified according to the default risk and credit risk. The lower the asset class, the higher coupon payments and default risk associated with them. Mortgage loans are one of the most common uses of asset-backed securities. By considering the borrower's creditworthiness, the asset-backed are classified as subprime or prime. A lot of people refinance their mortgages when interest rates decline, or pay off their mortgages ahead of time. Because of this reason asset-backed securities will often lose some assets, forcing the investor to find other securities to invest in. Another risk is foreclosure for defaulting borrowers.

Agency mortgages are secured by a government-sponsored organization or a federal agency. Non-agency mortgages are offered by private firms, and do not have such structured securities. They have higher returns because of the high risk involved.

A single monthly mortality rate (SMM) refers to the monthly repayments made on a specific mortgage pool. You arrive at this rate by dividing the prepayments by the outstanding pool balance for the mortgage. If you annualize the SMM, you get the conditional prepayment rate (CPR).

Asset-backed securities can also be funded through commercial mortgage-backed securities (CMBS). The credit risk for such securities is determined by the loan-to-value ratio (LTV) or the debt service coverage (DSC). Loans that have high values are risky and have a high chance of default. Since the commercial mortgage loans attract prepayment penalties, they have a lower prepayment risk. A collateralized debt obligation (CDO) is a security backed by a diversified portfolio of other CDOs, corporate bonds or asset backed securities.

Fixed Income Risk and Return

Fixed income security yields are derived from capital gains or losses, coupon payments and reinvestments from coupon payments if the bond is sold before its term. To determine the reinvestment coupon value, you have to find the future value of coupon payments from the yield to maturity. This is arrived at by determining the time value of money. The horizontal yield refers to the IRR between the total return and the par value of the security. Bond duration refers to the full value of the bond in relation to interest rate fluctuations over a given time. You can either have a yield duration or curve duration.

A yield duration refers to how sensitive the bond is to its discount rate, while the curve duration refers to how sensitive it is based on a predetermined benchmark, in most cases, set by the government. The duration can be calculated as follows:

Modified duration = Macaulay Duration / (1 + yield to maturity)

Key rate duration is a measure of the bond's responsiveness as the benchmark yield curve changes at different maturity points. For a normal coupon bond, the duration measures should not be higher than the time to maturity.

Credit Risk Analysis

Credit risk refers to the probability that the borrower will default on the principal and coupon payments. It is possible to recover some of the bond's par value since most of the defaults do not necessarily end up in complete loss.

A spread risk refers to the spread premium risk where securities trade compared to risk free bonds. If the spread risk increases, the value of the security falls. Market liquidity risk is the probability of struggling to trade an illiquid security at the fair value of the bond.

Downgrade risk, also known as a credit mitigation risk, is the probability of declining creditworthiness of the bond issuer. If this happens, there is a high chance the issuer might default on the bond.

Credit risk is arrived at by considering two factors, severity of the loss and default risk. Severity of the loss refers to part of the bond that is unrecoverable if the issuer defaults on the bond. Default risk is the risk that the issuer will be unable to honor their payments. Complete loss severity is a highly unlikely scenario, given that the bond's partial value is often recoverable in most defaults. Based on the values obtained, you can determine the expected loss as follows:

Expected loss = Loss severity * Default risk

In the same way we categorize equities, you can also have secure or unsecured bonds. A secured bond can be claimed against some assets.

In credit analysis, the following characteristics are used:

Capacity – this refers to the borrower's ability to honor their debt agreement.

Collateral – this refers to any assets offered as security against the debt.

Covenants – this refers to descriptions in the bond agreement that explain all the options available to the lender should the issuer default.

Character – this refers to an assessment of the borrower's trustworthiness, creditworthiness and reputation.

In credit analysis, it is important to establish the issuer's business performance and operating results over time, to determine their ability to continue operating as a going concern in the foreseeable future. For this purpose, cash flow statements and profitability reports are necessary. You must also look at the interest commitments and the issuer's current debt and leverage position. In the case of sovereign debt, it you must consider the issuing country's stability and political risk, economic trend and structure, and how flexible their monetary system is.

Practice Questions and Answers

1. The statements below describe floating rate notes. Which statement is the least unlikely?

S1 – The issuer's creditworthiness determines the spread on a floating rate note throughout the term of the bond.

S2 – Fixed rate bonds carry more risk compared to floating rate notes

A. Statement 2 is true

B. Statement 1 is true

C. Both statements are untrue

The correct answer is A

Fixed rate notes generally have a low interest rate compared to fixed rate bonds. This is because the coupon rate on fixed rate notes can be reset to align with the prevailing interest rates in the market. On a floating rate note, the spread is determined at the point of issue, according to the creditworthy rating of the issuer.

2. S1 - The principal amount and coupon rate for a capital index bond increases as the underlying index increases.

S2 – In a Bermuda call, the issuer is allowed to call bonds on a predetermined date after the call protection period lapses.

Which of the statements above is the least unlikely?

A. Statement 2 is true

B. Statement 1 is true

C. All the statements are true

The correct answer is A

In the case of bond that is capital-indexed, you apply a fixed coupon rate to the principal amount. This increases with a unique underlying index.

Because of this treatment, the coupon payments on the bond will also increase as the index increases. Therefore, the second statement is true.

3. Review the statements below. Which is the least unlikely statement?

S1 – Yields on certificates of deposit are primarily determined by assessing the creditworthiness of the issuing bank.

S2 – The value of the Euro commercial paper is determined by add-on yield terms

A. S1 and S2 are true

B. Only S1 is true

C. Only S2 is true

The correct answer is A

When investing in a certificate of deposit, the creditworthiness of the issuing bank will determine the yield on the investment over the term to maturity.

While US commercial papers are valued as discount instruments, Euro commercial papers are valued based on the add-on yields.

4. When investing in a putable bond offer, what is the least unlikely z-volatility spread?

A. Similar to the option-adjusted spread

B. Higher compared to the option-adjusted spread

C. Lower compared to the option-adjusted spread

The correct answer is C

The option-adjusted spread is generally higher than the z-spread in the case of putable bonds. The yield on this bond, therefore, will be less than the yield on a bond investment that is free of embedded options. This is to make sure that the bond issuer is compensated for the option they sell the buyer.

5. The information below concerns option free bonds. They both have a face value of $2,000, yield to maturity of 6% and they mature in 10 years. However, Bond A has a 5% annual coupon rate against an 8% annual coupon rate for Bond B. Assuming that through the rest of the term of the bonds the yield to maturity does not change, which of the bonds is likely to experience an increase in its underlying price?

A. Both Bond A and Bond B

B. Bond A

C. Bond B

The correct answer is B

From the information available, Bond A is currently trading in the market at a discount rate. This is because it has a low coupon rate compared with the discount rate. Bond B is trading in the market at a premium because it has a high coupon rate compared to the discount rate.

Assuming that the yields in the market are unchanged until maturity, the price of Bond A will increase as it gets closer to the face value.

6. The current yield on a bond is lower than the coupon rate of the bond. How is the bond trading in the market?

A. At par

B. At premium

C. At a discount

The correct answer is B

If the current yield is less than the coupon rate of the bond, the bond is trading at a premium to its face value.

7. The statements below describe sovereign bonds. Which statement is the most correct?

A. Sovereign bonds are often issued in a variety of forms, such as inflation-lined sovereign bonds and floating rate sovereign bonds

B. Sovereign bonds can only be issued in the domestic currency of the issuer

C. Sovereign bonds have the backing of the banking industry in the issuer's country

The correct answer is A

There are different types of sovereign bonds that can be issued, including inflation-linked bonds, fixed and floating rate bonds.

8. The information below is available about a converting bond.

Conversion ratio 50:1, Face value $1,000, Value of the converting bond is $1,050

The bond has a $50 conversion premium. What is the closest possible share price for the bond at the present moment?

A. $20.00

B. $30.00

C. $25.00

The correct answer is A

Since the convertible bond has a price of $1,050, applying the conversion premium means that the conversion value of the bond will be $1,000.

However, since we have a 50:1 conversion rate, the price of the bond per share becomes 1000 / 50, which is $20.

9. You are requested to determine the yield spread on an international corporate issue of a government bond. The bond yield can be determined using different spot rates to discount every single expected cash flow from the bond. Which of the following spreads are you most likely calculating?

A. I-spread

B. Z-spread

C. G-spread

The correct answer is B

Based on the information available, you are trying to determine the constant yield spread for the bond along a spot curve. This can be arrived at using the Z-spread.

10. The following information is usually found in a bond indenture. Which is the most unlikely information?

A. Issue price

B. Collateral

C. Credit enhancement

The correct answer is A

The issue price of a bond is found in the primary market. The issuer does not set the issue price. Therefore, this is the most unlikely information you will find in a bond indenture.

11. An investor buys a coupon bearing bond at face value. Assuming that they keep the bond until it matures, but interest in the market falls during the period, what is the true ex-post return?

A. Equal to the yield to maturity at the time they purchased the bond

B. Higher than the yield to maturity at the time they purchased the bond

C. Lower than the yield to maturity at the time they purchased the bond

The correct answer is C

Declining interest rates during the term of the bond results in a reduced return from reinvesting the income earned than the yield to maturity that was determined at the time the investor purchased the bond. For this reason, therefore, the real return on the bond will be less than the yield to maturity.

12. An asset-backed security portfolio is made up of loans. The following statements are true about

the issuer of the asset-backed securities. Which is the most correct?

A. The issuer purchases the loans

B. The issuer will service the loans

C. The issuer is the originator of the loans

The correct answer is A

Asset-backed securities are primarily special purpose vehicle investments. The issuer in this case purchases the loans from the originators or the loan seller, then they issue the asset-backed securities.

13. A manufacturing company is planning to issue bonds to raise capital so that they can expand their operations to the UK and Europe. In order to do this, the company issues bonds in GBP currency in the domestic UK market and the Eurobond market. What would be the best description of these bonds?

A. They are foreign bonds

B. They are global bonds

C. They are euro sterling bonds

The correct answer is B

The company issues the bond in the domestic market and the Eurobond market, making it a global bond.

14. Market information reveals that a bond is currently trading in the market at $90.50. Interest rates in the market fall by 20bp, which increase the price of the bond to $91.75. However, if the interest rates rise by 20bp, the price of the bond is

expected to drop to $89.50. what is the closest modified duration of the bond?

A. 4.25

B. 6.22

C. 2.25

The correct answer is B

Modified duration

= (91.75 − 89.50) / (2 x 90.50 x 0.002)

= 2.25 /0.362

= 6.22

15. The statements below represent repurchase agreements between a buyer and a seller. Which of the statements represents the least unlikely scenario between the investors?

A. The buyer alone is exposed to counterparty credit risk

B. The seller alone is exposed to counterparty credit risk

C. Because of an increasing credit risk in the collateral, the repo rates are expected to increase

The correct answer is C

This statement is true. The rate at which a repo seller is willing to borrow from the lender would increase with a decrease in the collateral quality.

16. The following statements concern the realized rate of return for an investor having purchased a corporate bond. They hope to hold the bond until it matures. The bond is not expected to default. At maturity, which of the following statements is true about the bond?

A. The investor purchased the bond at par value

B. It is a zero-coupon bond

C. The interest rates on the bond will remain stable

The correct answer is B

In this case, the investor is using the yield to maturity to determine the value of their investment. In this method, coupons are reinvested at the yield to maturity rate. Since a zero-coupon bond does not have coupons, the investor does not have a reinvestment risk.

17. The following phrases represent internal credit enhancements. Which one is the most unlikely?

A. Monoline insurance

B. Overcollateralization

C. Senior/subordinate structure

The correct answer is A

Monoline insurance is an example of a third-party external credit enhancement.

18. Equity linked note investments feature protected principals. Because of this reason, the investors in these investments are primarily safe from which of the following circumstances?

A. The issuer's credit risk

B. A drop in the value of the investment index from the moment of issue, and the issuer's credit risk

C. A drop in the value of the investment index from the moment of issue

The correct answer is C

The underlying feature of equity linked note investments is that investors are guaranteed 100% repayment of their principal sum invested, even if the prevailing price of the index falls from the moment of issue. That being said, however, it is important to realize that the principal amount will still be exposed to the issuer's credit risk. Therefore, should the issuer fail to honor their obligation, the investor might not receive any return. This is true even if the value of the underlying index increases.

19. Study the information available on the following bonds, and determine which of the three bonds is least unlikely to exhibit a high interest rate risk, based on the assumption that the yield curve for all the bonds is flat.

Bond X: 5.6% bond without embedded options, valid for 15 years

Bond Y: 6.2% bond without embedded options, valid for 18 years

Bond Z: 5% bond without embedded options, valid for 20 years

A. Bond X
B. Bond Z
C. Bond Y

The correct answer is B

Assuming a flat yield curve, Bond Z has the highest interest rate. This is because it has the lowest coupon rate compared to the other bonds, and it also has the longest maturity term.

20. The information below is applicable to a repo. Which is the least unlikely of the two?

S1 –The repo margin is meant to offer protection to sellers in case the collateral value declines in the course of the term of the repo.

S2 – Coupon incomes earned from bonds through the term of the repo are owned by the buyer

A. All the statements mentioned are false

B. Statement 1 is true

C. Statement 2 is true

The correct answer is A

All coupon income that investors earn from a bond during the repo term are owned by the borrower (the seller).

In this type of investment, the repo margin is offered to shield the lender from a loss of value in the collateral through the term of the repo.

21. The statements below describe a currency option bond. Which statement is the least inaccurate?

A. Bondholders have a choice of one of two currencies in terms of principal amount payments and coupon payments

B. A coupon option bond only allows payments in one currency for coupons and another currency for the principal payment

C. Bondholders are allowed principal payments and coupon payments in different currencies, but only at the prevailing interest rate for the currencies involved.

The correct answer is B

Currency options allow investors the chance of getting their coupon payments and principal payments in one of two currencies

22. The information presented below is concerning the tax behavior of bonds. Which statement is the most unlikely?

A. Some bonds are exempted from taxes

B. The claim on capital loss during the year the bond was purchased is purchased at a premium rate

C. The zero-coupon bonds are liable to annual interest income tax payable

The correct answer is B

This statement is not true. Investors can only claim capital loss once the bond matures or after the bond is sold. In some countries, however, investors are allowed to amortize the cost of capital losses in order to offset any income earned during the year, or in case they purchased the securities at premium rate.

Chapter 9: Derivatives

A derivative is a class of assets whose value depends on another asset, hence the term derivative. The underlying asset to which derivatives get their value can be a real asset or financial asset. Derivatives allow an investor to trade in an asset without purchasing the asset. It is, therefore a binding long and short contract between a buyer and seller respectively.

Forward commitments allow the investor to purchase an asset in the future at a predetermined price. A contingent claim is an option but not an obligation to contract, so its payoff depends on the decision of the buyer.

Derivatives are traded OTC or in an exchange. Standardization is one of the benefits of trading derivatives in an exchange. Given the requirements of exchanges, such trades are transparent. In an OTC however, investors can enjoy more flexibility because buyers and sellers can negotiate agreements.

Forward commitments exist as swaps, futures contracts, and forward contracts. Forward contract payoffs can be calculated as follows:

Buyer = $St - F0\ (T)$

Seller = $-(St - F0\ (T))$

St implies the value of the underlying asset at the expiry of the contract.

$F0\ (T)$ implies the price at which the asset is purchased.

Futures contracts share a number of similarities with forward contracts. While the investor can purchase an underlying asset at a predetermined price, they particularly traded on an exchange. Losses and gains are settled on the exchange. If you make a loss, you settle the difference with the exchange in cash. This concept is referred to as mark-to-market, and it is intended to protect investors from counterparty risk in the unlikely event that one of the investors is declared bankrupt while still in debt. Their payoff formula is similar to the payoff formula for forwards above.

A swap contract is an agreement where two investors agree to exchange cash flows. They are highly custom agreements and are traded OTC.

Investors commonly exchange floating rate payments for fixed rate payments, also referred to as a plain vanilla swap.

Options contracts are contingent claim securities. A call option is a right to buy, while a put option is a right to sell an underlying asset at a predetermined time and price (strike price), but the investor is not obligated to do so. The payoff is derived as follows:

Buyer = Max (0, St – X) - c0

Seller = - Max (0, St – X) +c0

In this formula, St refers to the value of the underlying asset, c0 represents the premium value, and X is the strike price.

In the worst possible scenario, the investor can only lose the premium. The same formulas apply for a put option but the St and X values are reversed.

A credit derivative is contingent claim meant to protect buyers in the event of an unforeseen credit. One of these is a total return swap where the buyer pays an agreed interest rate while the seller agrees to pay the capital and interest of the security.

Market stability and credibility is established through arbitrage. Arbitrage ensures that an asset is traded at the same price irrespective of the domicile. One of the main differences investors experience when determining the value of their trades is that while other asset classes assume a risk aversion, derivatives operate on a risk neutral platform.

Practice Questions and Answers

1. Which of the following statements gives a true explanation of the value of a forward contract at the time of expiry?
A. Value of the asset less the forward price
B. Value of the asset plus the forward price
C. Value of the asset less the present value of the forward price
The correct answer is A
At contract expiry, the value of a forward contract is equivalent to the asset value less the forward price.
2. The statements below describe procedures for constructing a synthetic zero-coupon, risk-free bond. Which statement is the most unlikely to be untrue?
A. Short the put option and long the underlying stock and the call option
B. Short the call and long the underlying stock and the put option
C. Short the underlying stock, and long the call and put options
The correct answer is B
The following formula applies for creating a synthetic zero-coupon risk-free bond:
$$X / (1 + Rf)T = P - C + S$$
This translates to going long on the underlying stock and put option, and shorting the call option.
3. A put option is currently selling for $16 with an exercise price of $142 while the price of the underlying asset is $148. What is the highest possible return an investor will make if they invest

in this option? What is the breakeven price for the underlying asset at the time the option expires?

A. Maximum return $132   Breakeven point $126

B. Maximum return $126   Breakeven point $126

C. Maximum return $126   Breakeven point $132

The correct answer is B

The maximum return available to the investor

=142 − 16

= $126

Breakeven point at expiry

= 142 − 16

= $126

4. The following statements describe the features of derivative markets in relation to spot markets.

Which statement is most likely true?

A. Derivative markets are illiquid

B. Derivative markets provide investors with short options and easy leverage access

C. Derivative markets involve very high transaction costs

The correct answer is B

Investors in derivative markets often enjoy short positions and access to leverage facilities.

5. Which of the following statements most unlikely describes a characteristic of the price of a derivative instrument:

A. The price is a function of an investor's risk aversion

B. The price is a function of the risk-free rate

C. The price is a function of the characteristics of the underlying asset

The correct answer is A

In the derivatives market, the price of an investment instrument usually depends on the unique features of the underlying asset, the risk-free rate and the characteristics of the derivative instrument itself. The price is not a function of an investor's risk aversion or any other risk profile.

6. Assuming all the other factors are held constant, what is the least unlikely effect of an increase in volatility of an underlying asset?

A. The price of puts and calls will increase

B. The price of puts will decrease but the price of calls will increase

C. The price of puts will decrease and the price of calls will decrease

The correct answer is A

Increased market volatility usually increases the prices of both puts and calls

7. One of your investment clients needs to know the best forward rate at which they should hedge a 180-day loan starting in 90 days. The following information is available at the moment. 270-day LIBOR is 3.10%, 180-day LIBOR is 3.05% and a 90-day LIBOR is 2.88%

A. 2.01%

B. 4.01%

C. 4.82%

The correct answer is B

The best decision is to go short on the 90-day rate and long on the 270-day rate

Forward rate 180

= [1 + 3.10% (270 / 360) / 1 + 2.88% (90 / 360)] –
1
= (0.77325 / 0.2572) – 1
= 2.006%
Forward rate
= 2.006% x (360 / 270 – 90)
= 4.01%

8. The following statements describe an argument between two investors concerning American put and call options.

Investor 1 – There is no reason for you to exercise an American put option early enough

Investor 2 – There is no reason for you to exercise an American call option early enough

From the statements above, which of the investors' decisions is least unlikely in the event that the underlying asset is a stock that is not expected to pay dividends?

A. Investor 1 and 2 are wrong
B. Investor 1 and 2 are right
C. Only investor 1 is wrong

The correct answer is C

In the case of a dividend paying stock, at times it makes sense to exercise your American option earlier than the expiration date. However, there is no reason for you to exercise a call option on a stock that doesn't pay dividends before the expiration date.

The only reason why you might consider exercising your American put option before the expiry date is if the company is close to bankruptcy, or if the company has been declared bankrupt.

9. Which of the following refers to a credit derivative instrument where the credit protection buyer makes frequent payments on a regular basis to a credit protection seller, while the seller on the other hand does not make any payment until a credit event arises?

A. Credit default swap

B. Credit linked note

C. Total return swap

The correct answer is A

The description above identifies a credit default swap. This is a derivative where the seller is not expected to make any payment until a credit event happens. The credit protection buyer, on the other hand, must keep making frequent regular payments according to an agreed schedule to the credit protection seller.

10. Perry Investments normally plays the vanilla interest swap as a fixed rate player. Since the beginning of the swap, the interest rates have been on a free fall. The statements below indicate the position of Perry Investments. Which is the most likely position?

A. The swap fixed rate will fall

B. The swap becomes an asset for Perry Investments

C. The present value of the fixed rate payments becomes higher than the present value of the floating rate payments

The correct answer is C

In this market, the fixed rate payments are unchanged. The floating rate payments, on the other hand, decline as the interest rate plummets.

11. An investor is selling their call option for $45 on a stock in their possession already. The exercise price for this option is $875, but the stock is currently trading in the market at $872. What is the closest breakeven point for the investor?

A. $830

B. $827

C. $828.50

The correct answer is B

The breakeven point for a covered call strategy
= $872 - $45
= $827

12. An underlying security is currently valued at $10.56. A put option is available on the underlying asset at an exercise price of $10.62, with a premium of $0.04. What is the current trading position of the put option?

A. The put option is in the money

B. The put option is out of the money

C. The put option is at the money

The correct answer is A

The underlying spot price is lower than the put option's exercise price, so the put option is in the money.

13. Which of the following statements represents the least unlikely method of reducing the cost of a protective put option?

A. Implementing the collar strategy and selling a call option
B. Implementing the insurance strategy and selling the stock
C. Implementing the covered call strategy and going short on the call position
The correct answer is A
The cost of a protective put option can be reduced if the investor sells their call option. This is called the collar strategy.
14. An investor might be warranted to exercise their American option earlier than the expiry date if which of the following statements is true?
A. They own a put option which is in the money
B. They own a stock call option
C. They realize the option has a significant carry cost
The correct answer is B
It is unwise to exercise an American option before the expiry date. However, if a stock is going to be ex-dividend, exercising a call option on it early might be a good idea.

Chapter 10: Alternative Investments
This section in the exam will test your understanding of alternative investments, including real estate, private equity, commodities, infrastructure, and hedge funds. You will distinguish their unique features and learn how to include them in your portfolio.

Alternative investments are a great way of diversifying your portfolio to earn great returns, especially in private wealth and institutional portfolios. Investors seek relative or absolute return in these investments.

Investors seeking absolute returns hope their investment will yield positive returns all through the trading period. However, alternative investments carry risk like other investments. Therefore, the returns can be relative to traditional investments, positive or negative. Investors seeking relative returns hope their investment will yield a relative return in respect of a specific benchmark, either fixed income or equity.

The following are some of the characteristics typically expected of alternative investments:

Unique tax and legal implications

Low return correlation with traditional investments

Limited historical return or risk data available

Underlying assets are illiquid

Less transparency compared to traditional investments

Less regulation compared to traditional investments

Returns to Alternative Investments

Managers can invest in the market actively or passively. Active investments recognize market inefficiencies, and exploit them, adjust for risk, and earn positive returns. Passive investments assume markets are efficient, and use beta return drivers to calculate systematic risk. Investment strategies can be classified as follows:

Absolute returns

Strategies used in absolute investments yield returns independent of the market. As a result, these investments don't have to be better than any market index. Their betas are set as close to zero as possible.

Market segmentation

Segmentation happens as a result of restrictions on asset managers, preventing the flow of capital from a low to an area of high return anticipation. The portfolios are exposed to different levels of constraints, including governing policies, social, and environmental challenges. Therefore, this also creates different opportunities because it is easier for portfolio managers with fewer limitations to move into high return markets than managers operating under higher constraints.

Concentrated portfolio

This is a strategy of reducing diversification by consolidating different assets to fewer managers, securities and strategies. The objective is to attempt outperforming the market, hence higher returns for the investor.

Investment structures

Most alternative investments involve the investors as limited partners and the fund managers as the general partners. Investors entrust their investment to general partners who bear unlimited liability over the investment. To mitigate the risk of unlimited liability, general partners often operate as limited liability corporations. Funds attract a management fee in lieu of the managed assets, and a performance or incentive fee on the returns earned.

Categories of Alternative Investments

Given the range of characteristics of alternative investments mentioned above, it is difficult to have a definitive list of alternative investments. That being said, however, the following are the widely accepted categories of alternative investments:

Hedge funds

Private equity funds

Commodities

Real estate

Infrastructure

Other investments

Hedge funds

These are derivative positions and security portfolios managed by private investors using different investment strategies. They are managed in long or short positions with the goal of delivering the best performance for investors irrespective of the general market performance.

Features of hedge funds

The fund aims to deliver high yield against a market benchmark, or a market absolute, and have very few restrictions.

Investment redemption is limited. The investors' money is held in the fund for a lockup period before they can redeem shares or withdraw from the fund.

The fund is an investment portfolio spanning different classes of assets that may use derivatives, and takes short and long positions in the market.

They are only open to investors willing to make a sizeable initial investment, hence set up as private investment partnerships.

Strategies for investing in hedge funds

Hedge funds are primarily defined by the investment strategies used. These strategies are dynamic and respond to new opportunities and products in the market. The classification is important to investors in the following ways:

Choosing reliable performance benchmarks

Determine the best way to build their portfolios

Help them review performance data

Private Equity Funds

These are funds invested in companies that are either unlisted on exchanges, or listed companies they plan to privatize. Private equity funds invest in companies that have the best management, quality products or services, and a strong customer backing. Today many private equity funds run venture capitals, where they invest in start-ups or infant companies that have a good future potential.

Commodities

These are investments in companies that produce commodities like crude oil or grains, or invest in the products themselves. Investment in this market is through commodity index-backed funding, or futures contracts.

Real estate

Investing in real estate implies investing directly or indirectly in land or buildings. The real estate market has grown and diversified over the years, and other than land and buildings, it now includes public real estate debt and equity, and private commercial real estate debt and equity.

Infrastructure

These investments are real, tangible projects like schools, dams, or roads which involve lots of capital. Primarily, these assets are invested into by governments. However, the private-public partnerships are becoming popular, with governments inviting private investors into infrastructure investments.

Other investments

There are other categories of alternative investments that are not widely defined, which might be intangible, like patents, or tangible in the case of coins, stamps, antiques, art, and wine.

Practice Questions and Answers

1. In the event of a financial crisis, what happens to the correlation between hedge funds and the financial market performance?

A. The correlation becomes zero

B. The correlation reduces

C. The correlation increases

The correct answer is C

The correlation between hedge funds and financial market performance will increase in the event of a financial crisis.

2. Below are hedge fund strategies commonly used in the market. Which one would be least unlikely to represent volatility?

A. Equity hedge strategies

B. Event driven strategies

C. Relative value strategies

The correct answer is C

Volatility strategies are usually classified as relative value strategies because they are used to take advantage of existing price differentials in the market.

3. Apart from charging management fees, what other fees will unlikely be charged in a leveraged buyout?

A. Underwriting fees

B. Incentive fees

C. Penalty if the deal does not go through

The correct answer is A

Underwriting fees are paid to investment banks when new securities are issued. A leveraged buyout does not involve underwriting fees, as the buyer is privatizing the company.

4. Which of the following is the most unlikely example of distressed investing?

A. Real estate strategies

B. Private equity strategies

C. Hedge fund strategies

The correct answer is A

Distressed investing is one of the hedge fund strategies and it is categorized as an event-driven strategy. Common private equity strategies include leveraged buyout, distressed investing, development capital and venture capital.

5. Which of the following hedge fund strategies are duly recognized by HFRI?

A. Event-driven, relative value, market neutral, equity driven strategies

B. Event-driven, equity hedge, relative value and macro strategies

C. Equity driven, arbitrage, market neutral, hedge strategies

The correct answer is B

The HFRI recognizes only four hedge fund categories, and these are:

Macro strategies

Relative value strategies

Event-driven strategies

Equity hedge strategies

6. Palmieri Funds Inc are managing a small hedge fund. The company has built credible data models and data sets that have enabled them to perform well in the market over the years. Based on their data models, the fund managers focus on finding securities of companies that are just restructuring their operational activities. What type of hedge fund strategy is the company using?

A. Macro strategy

B. Relative value strategy

C. Event-driven strategy

The correct answer is C

The company is using an event-driven strategy because by actively seeking companies that are restructuring, they hope to generate revenue by looking for companies that are experiencing specific events.

7. What is the roll yield in the market for a commodity that is in backwardation?
A. The roll yield is positive
B. The roll yield is negative
C. There is no roll yield
The correct answer is A
If the futures market is going through backwardation, the spot price is higher than the futures price. As a result, investors can look forward to a positive roll yield because the futures price is converging close to the spot price.

8. The following statements describe common features of alternative investments. Which one is not true?
A. Wide manager specialization
B. Limited access to historical data on returns
C. Large size of investments
The correct answer is A
Generally, managers who specialize in alternative investments have a unique understanding, skills, and knowledge of the alternative investment market.

9. The risk return measures below are associated with alternative investments. Which one is least suitable?
A. Safety-first risk
B. Sortino ratio
C. Sharpe ratio
The correct answer is C

The Sharpe ratio is not suitable for measuring risk and return in alternative investments because of the following reasons:

The investments are largely illiquid

Unlike other investments, returns on alternative investments are not distributed normally

Sharpe ratio is best applicable where the valuation of the underlying investments can be performed through observable transaction prices. Most of the alternative investments are valued through estimation.

10. Momentum Investment is one of the leading private equity management firms in London. One of the investments in their successful portfolio is a bioengineering company that has been extremely successful over the years. Having rode the success of the bioengineering company, Momentum Investment is planning to walk away from the company for strategic reasons. Assuming relatively high interest rates and a buoyant market, what is the least unlikely strategy for Momentum Investment to exit their position?

A. Recapitalization

B. Trade sale

C. Liquidation

The correct answer is B

A trade sale would be the best idea for Momentum Investment because exiting such a position requires a strategic buyer with significantly large financial endowment, like a big tech company.

Conclusion

Sitting for the CFA exam is not an experience the faint hearted would consider. The exam offers you a platform to more than just a charter. It is a life-changing experience. If you are already employed in the finance industry, this will be a good boost for your career, especially if you are looking towards career development and more importantly, if you need to expand your expertise and position yourself as one of the elite experts in financial matters.

As you prepare for the exam, you will come across a lot of information about the pass rates, how difficult the exam is, and so forth. This should not break your heart. Remember that while some people struggle to pass, there are many others who have passed before, and have grown from strength to strength and succeeded in every level. You can do the same, too.

The first thing you need to do is to understand how the exam is structured. The CFA exam is specifically organized, so you don't need to worry about confusion as you prepare for the exam. You are aware of the topic structure and the weight each topic carries. This will help you prepare adequately for the exam.

While reading through the topics, you might have realized the ones that you are very strong at and those that you are struggling with. Make sure you use your strong points as a booster to help you pull your weight in the other sections. How do those who pass the CFA exams do it? Well, it takes dedication, organization, and commitment to the cause.

This book is uniquely organized to help you remember the key points in each chapter. You have summary notes that are useful especially when revising for the exam as you get closer to the final examination date. The summary notes are structured in a simple, and easy to remember way. They help refresh your memory and get you in the right frame of mind.

In each chapter, you have sample questions and answers right after the summary notes. The questions and answers are examination style, so as you are revising them, they help you get your mind in the right frame for the exam, too. Read and understand the questions before attempting.

Many of the questions have two features. First, the question is about the content you are being asked to respond to. The second part of the question is the logical element. You might have the correct answer, but fail to get it right because you missed the logic. This is why you must be very keen when reading the questions. The logic bit can be confusing. The examiners carefully insert phrases like most unlikely, least likely, least incorrect or least unlikely. These phrases can change the meaning of a question. In the multiple-choice answers provided, you might also find two or more answers that are all correct, depending on your interpretation of the logic part of the question.

All the modules you will cover in CFA Level 1 are covered in this book. You have questions, answers, and examples. Remember to focus on the weight of each section. The sections that are heaviest are the ones you need to spend more time on. These sections contain a lot of information. They also pertain to most of the challenges you will experience in the world of financial investment on a daily basis. Your understanding of these sections, therefore, transcends passing the exam, and is heavily leveraged in your ability to make sound investment decisions on a daily basis for your firm and clients.

Ethical and professional standards, equity investments, quantitative methods, economics and fixed income investments are the sections that will demand a lot of your attention. As you read this book, pay attention to these sections. At the same time, try not to ignore the other sections because they are equally important.

Many people start their CFA Level 1 and fail, and give up on the charter altogether. This is because they did not have the right support to get them through. If you have undertaken a finance course before, all the information you will come across as you prepare for your exams will not be alien to you. This is knowledge you already possess. The CFA guide is here to help you remember and know what information you should draw upon when you are in the exam room.

Passing your CFA Level 1 examination is one of the best things that will ever happen in your life. We are glad to be helping you make the first of many steps towards becoming one of the best financial investors in the world. When you pass the first level, you feel encouraged and energized to pursue the second level and proceed until you complete all the levels.

Beyond passing the exam, you are opening up your life to amazing opportunities in the world of finance and investments, professional and personal growth, and more importantly as a professional, you are expanding your skills and knowledge.

Good luck as you prepare for your exam.

CPSIA information can be obtained
at www.ICGtesting.com
Printed in the USA
LVHW022101220221
679613LV00004B/127

9 781617 044342